WISDOM
of the
ELEMENTS

WISDOM
of the
ELEMENTS

The Sacred Wheel
of Earth, Air, Fire, and Water

MARGIE MCARTHUR

THE CROSSING PRESS
FREEDOM, CALIFORNIA

Copyright © 1998 by Margie McArthur
Cover design by Victoria May
Cover art by Ishana Ingerman and Gabrielle Laney
Interior design by Magnolia Studio and Victoria May
Printed in the U.S.A.

For information on bulk purchases or group discounts for this and other Crossing Press titles, please contact our Special Sales Manager at 800-777-1048.
Visit our Web site on the Internet: www.crossingpress.com

Library of Congress Cataloging-in-Publication Data

McArthur, Margie.
    Wisdom of the elements : the sacred wheel of earth, air, fire, and
water / by Margie McArthur.
        p. cm.
    Includes bibliographical references and index.
    ISBN 0-89594-936-9 (pbk.)
    1. Four elements (Philosophy)--Miscellanea. 2. Medicine wheels-
-Miscellanea. 3. Magic. I. Title.
BF1623.M43M33   1998
299'.93--dc21   98-24643
                                     CIP

ACKNOWLEDGMENTS

My heartfelt thanks go out to the following people who have
given this project assistance in a variety of ways:

JoAnn Aelfwine, Dolores Ashcroft-Nowicki, Sun Bear, Linda Boyer, Alana Graham, John Hock, Kyla Houbolt, Ishana Ingerman, Palden Jenkins, Ellias Lonsdale, Nicholas McArthur, Abigail McArthur, Steven McFadden, Brooke Medicine Eagle, Hunbatz Men, Buryl Payne, Sara Rajan, R.J. & Josephine Stewart, Swan & Hyemeyohsts Storm, Michael and Lesley Tierra, all my Wicca 101 students.

*This work is dedicated to the Powers of the Directions,
and to the Elements of Air, Fire, Water, and Earth.*

*By the power of Air,
I send it forth on the Winds.*

*By the power of Fire,
may it create illumination,
causing perception and appreciation for Life.*

*By the power of Water,
may it deepen our love for Life and Mother Earth,
bringing renewal of purpose and dedication.*

*By the power of Earth,
may it bring manifestation of these in the form of balance,
harmony, and service to Life's Hearthfire.*

So mote it be!

Contents

MEDITATIONS, JOURNEYS, RITUALS, AND EXERCISES

LIST OF TABLES AND WHEELS

INTRODUCTION

The Wheel of the Year and the Wheel of the Elements

This book about the Elements begins most appropriately with a discussion of the glyph or symbol of the Sacred Circle, also known as the Sacred Wheel, since an understanding of this glyph is crucial to understanding many things—not only the Wheel of the Year and the placement of the Sabbats upon it, but also the Elemental correspondences of each of the Directions on the Wheel.

In this day and age, when even our time-pieces—previously circular and with pointers that moved in circular fashion—have become linear and digitalized, we are in danger of losing touch with the valuable truth of the sacred roundness of time and of life.

The symbol of the circle is used in many ways and in many cultures to describe relationships within a world view. A circle has no real point of beginning or end, save that which is arbitrarily chosen; therefore, it truly represents the eternal return—things coming around again and again. Only in an abstract glyph, however, can a circle ever come back around again to the exact same place. Things are always just a bit different: each spring is a bit different from the one before and after it. The planets have moved to different locations in the sky, providing a unique, new, astrological significance. Over very long periods of time even the sun is seen to rise within a different grouping of stars on that particular day we call the Spring Equinox, a phenomenon known as the Precession of the Equinoxes. All the while, our entire solar sys-

tem (indeed, our entire galaxy) is traveling with great speed through the vast reaches of our expanding universe, looking quite like an elongated spiral as it does so. Spirals become circles that become spirals that become circles. The Spiral of Existence becomes the Circle of Life, and the Circle of Life becomes the Spiral of Existence. Although we use the glyph of the circle in describing relationships within our world view, it is wise to bear in mind that a circle can be thought of as containing a spiral within it—as spherical container of spiraling motion; and a spiral can be thought of as containing a circle within it—or at least, as of generating a circle with its particular motion.

In Native American traditions the Sacred Circle is called the Sacred Hoop, or Medicine Wheel. The Medicine Wheel is viewed as a mirror of the universe, and it is known that many Medicine Wheels make up the larger Medicine Wheel that is the mirror of the universe. All are reflections of the many parts of the whole: the universe. The Sacred Circle referred to within this book—that of the Directions/Elements/Seasons—compares to the first and most basic of the Medicine Wheels taught in some Native American traditions, which refer to it to as the Earth Wheel or the Children's Count, being the first and most obvious of the Medicine Wheels, and the one first taught to young children.

This way of looking at things is not unique to the Native Americans. Indeed, one has only to study the mandalas of Eastern Traditions, such as the Tibetan (and perhaps, to stretch it a bit further, the sephiroth of the Tree of Life of the Qabala), to see similar attempts to describe the relationship of parts to the whole of our universe.

The fact that the earth encircles the sun, with its axis tilted just so, creates the seasons of the year. The fact that the earth spins upon its axis while encircling the sun (thus showing all sides of itself to the sun as it bathes in the sun's life-giving rays) creates the day and night.

THE WHEELS

Like many other earth-religions, the Craft (the Neopagan Earth Religion of Witchcraft, also known as Wicca, but often just as "The Craft") uses the circle to describe relationships within its world view, and there exist many relationships thus described.

WHEEL OF THE YEAR

One of these is referred to as the Wheel of the Year, wherein the seasons of the year and the eight ritual occasions of the year, called the Sabbats, are laid out upon it. In so doing, the individual energies of these eight occasions are shown, and their relationship to each other and to the wholeness of the year, becomes apparent.

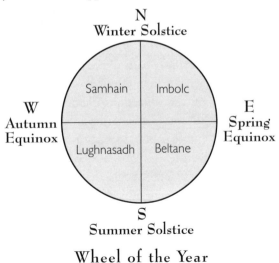

Wheel of the Year

WHEEL OF THE SEASONS

Immediately obvious are the four Seasons of the Year, and their relationship to both the Four Directions and the eight ceremonial occasions.

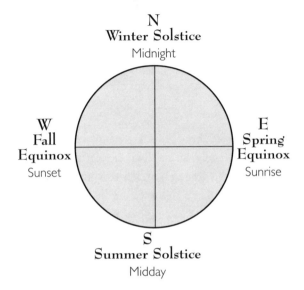

Wheel of the Seasons

WHEEL OF THE DAY

The glyph of the circle may also be used to describe the Circle or Wheel of the Day (Sunrise, Noon, Sunset, Midnight). The Circle or Wheel of the Day is a harmonic of the Circle or Wheel of the Year.

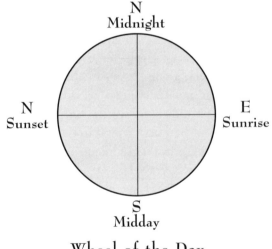

Wheel of the Day

WHEEL OF THE FOUR ELEMENTS AND DIRECTIONS

The Four Elements also have their places on the Wheel; study of their positioning reveals much about their relationship to each other.

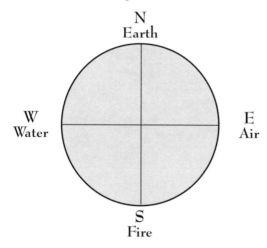

Wheel of the Four Elements
and Directions

WHEEL OF THE STAGES OF LIFE

Finally, the glyph of the circle may be used to plot the different stages of our lives on the Wheel of the Stages of Life: birth and youth, the ripeness of adulthood, the harvest of maturity, and elderhood—the time when the aging process brings us wisdom as it also moves us towards completion of this life's journey and the gateway of death.

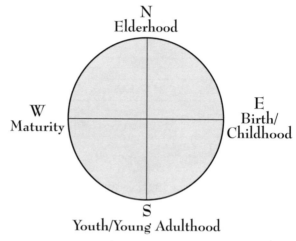

Wheel of the Stages of Life

Wheel of the Elemental Correspondences

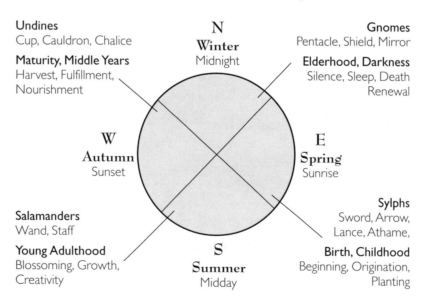

Elemental Correspondences

ELEMENT	AIR	FIRE	WATER	EARTH
Direction	East NE to SE	South SE to SW	West SW to NW	North NW to NE
Season of the Year	Spring	Summer	Autumn	Winter
Time of the Day	Morning	Midday	Evening	Night
Name of Spirit	Sylphs	Salamanders	Undines	Gnomes
Magical Tools	Sword, Athame, Lance, Arrow	Wand, Spear, Staff	Cauldron, Cup, Bowl, Chalice	Pentacle, Mirror, Shield
Sabbats Major and Minor	Imbolc, Spring Equinox	Beltane, Summer Solstice	Lughnasadh, Autumn Equinox	Samhain, Winter Solstice
Part of Cycle	Beginning	Growth	Ripeness, Harvest	Ending
Stage of Life	Birth/Childhood	Youth/Adulthood	Maturity/Middle Years	Elderhood/Old Age, Death
Qualities	beginning origination, planting	blossoming, creativity, growth	nourishment, fulfillment, harvest	sleep, silence, darkness, death, renewal

The table above and the Wheel of Elemental Correspondences on page 17 bring together this information about the day wheel, year wheel, seasonal wheel, and the energies of the seasons. Here one may see the relationship between the four elements and the four directions, as well as the name of the elemental spirit and magical tool related to each. Qualities associated with each of these directions/elements are also shown. These are well worth studying; shown here in simple form is essential information about the Craft and the Craft's world view. These relationships will come up often throughout the book.

ENERGY MOVEMENTS

Inherent in all this discussion of positioning of things around a circle is the fact of *movement*. The earth turns, spinning upon its axis. Day shifts to night, then night turns into day again. Spring becomes Summer, which becomes Fall, which becomes Winter. Everything moves, changes, broadens, deepens, heightens. All these cycles serve to remind us of the relationship potentialities within circles and spirals.

Our journey around the Great Wheel of Life takes many energy pathways. Sometimes we seem to just go around, day to day, season to season. Sometimes it seems we are flashing across the Wheel, side to side, up and down. There is meaning in the nature of these differing movements. The circular movement is feminine: it describes, defines, and creates a space. The flashing motion is more masculine: it thrusts outward in a fluctuation of the previous, circular, contained pattern. One might say one represents *Measure* and the other *Movement.* Both are needed for life to manifest. This *Movement,* the deviation from the circular, is the "change" that is the beginning of creation/manifestation.

It is fascinating to observe and experience the relationship between patterns of energy movement and shapes that manifest. Scientists tell us that everything is made of waves and that all wave shapes are really just arrangements of one wave shape, the Sine, or S-shaped wave. Earthquake motion frequently travels in S-shaped waves. Think of the S that divides the Chinese Yin/Yang symbol and the movement of snakes, with their long, venerable history as representatives of the undulating, female power of creation.

We have already spoken a bit about the relationship between circles and spirals. A circle has no beginning or end, things move around it, and around it again. This is constant, circling, ever-returning motion. The circle defines a space. We can add dimension here if we wish and see the circle as a sphere. But primarily, the circular shape creates boundaries—it defines and contains, and allows movement to occur in a regular, predictable, recurring manner. Circles feel comfortable, with their protective familiarity and recurrence, they are like wombs allowing space for growth and creativity to occur, for structures to be formed within.

Positioning the Four Elements on the wheel creates the Circle of the Elements, and in so doing we create the world of matter/manifestation by bringing in the forces of Air, Fire, Water, and Earth. Positioning the Elements on the Circle in actuality creates a square within the Wheel of Life. A square has four equal sides, thus its qualities are those of balance, stability, and form. To "Square the Circle," then, means to make manifest, and to bring boundaries, form, stability, and balance to the Circle's endless, constant movement. Some might see this as bringing order from chaos; I see it as another level of measure arising from movement.

Spirals and Spinning

The spiral has similarities to the circle but it also involves dimension. The spiral brings in the factors of height and depth, inward and outward, approaching and receding motion (relative to a center point).

The spiral brings time into space. Movements of up and down, in and out, approaching and receding, depict not only movement within space, but imply passage of time as well. If the circle defines space, then the spiral is the shape of the movement, perhaps the primary movement, occurring within that space. If the circle's defining of space is about circumference, then a spiral is about movement relative to the circle's center point—center to circumference and back again—as well as a simultaneous upward and downward movement.

It seems to me that the spiral is the template, or movement-pattern/shape for life in this galaxy. DNA molecules exhibit a spiral shape. Seashells, snail shells, pine cones, and flower petals around a stem reveal spiral patterning. Seeds spiral their way out of their seed casings as they burst into life and growth. The center of the spiral may be seen as the place from which the life-creating power of the universe bursts from numinous reality to space-time reality.

Related to the spiral is, of course, spinning, which is the basis of all life. The spinning of the Earth creates its gravity and electromagnetic field. Gravity and Earth's electromagnetic field are what hold us together, creating density and physicality. Our chakras spin, their spiraling motion bringing energy into us from the nonmaterial realms. The dictionary definition of spinning includes concepts of both the drawing forth action, and the twisting, twirling, whirling motion that occurs when thread or yarn is spun from rough, unformed fibers.

Spinning, then, is the movement path that energy follows on its journey from the nonmaterial to the material realm, from the spirit world into the physical life. Is it any wonder that our ancestors danced, circled, and spiraled around their sacred fires, world trees, and within their stone circles? To circle or spiral dance in this way is to participate in the dance of life, the dance that brings energy into physical manifestation; to participate with the greater powers of the universe in the creation of life.

Shamans, witches, druids, and magicians all seek to draw energy from the nonphysical into the physical realm, to make manifest, to bend, shape, and mold reality. What an awesome responsibility this entails!

Think of witches stirring cauldrons or dancing in circles to raise and focus power, or of the Sufi dancers called whirling dervishes. All these give rise to an image of a circle with the power of the unmanifest flowing into manifestation from its center. I am reminded of European stories and legends of spinning goddesses, or goddesses of the thread such as Holle, Perchta, Freya, Frigg, Athene, Arachne, and Ariadne, who spun or who had dominion over the realm of spinning/weaving.

The spinning of fibers was, of course, a vital and integral part of everyday life not so very long ago, but the beliefs, customs, and lore associated with it are remnants of a far older, half-forgotten knowledge of She Who Spins Life Into and Out of Being as She turns the Wheel of Time.

Particularly revealing in this regard are the legends of the Teutonic Goddess Holle (also known as Holda, Hulda, Harke, Berta, and Perchta) recounted by the Brothers Grimm in their *Teutonic Mythology.* They tell us that Holle, who made her rounds at the Winter Solstice traveling in a golden wheeled cart, was quite concerned with spinning. As she made her rounds she checked to be sure that all spinning implements were in order, and that the spinning was of good quality, but also to be certain that all spinning—and anything else that depended on rotary motion—was stopped for the time between Yule and New Year's Day (sometimes Twelfth Night). An old saying held that, "from Yule till new Year's day neither wheel nor windlass must go 'round." Obviously this custom was related to the Winter Solstice, the longest night (pretty long in the far North) when all spinning motion must cease in honor of and in harmony with the earth's apparent stoppage of motion. After New Year's Day (or Twelfth Night), spinning motion could begin again. A new cycle of life had begun, was being

"spun." The Goddess here reveals herself to be a goddess of time and of motion, particularly the spinning, revolving motion of the seasons, which seem to turn around the light/dark pivot points of the axis of the year. Her power is seen to be that of the circle and the spiral, of spinning and turning, and of the passage of time. Thus She is the power of *manifestation:* power flowing from the Unmanifest to the Manifest world.

LIGHTNINGFLASH

There is one more energy movement I should mention here, the one I refer to as the Lightningflash. I have observed this movement at work during the more intense spiritual experiences of my life. Afterwards, I would frequently come upon a picture of, or reference to a flash of lightning, as if the universe wanted to make sure I really "got it." Once, during a time in my life when the universe must have thought I was being particularly thick-skulled, I was even treated to a spectacular lightning display (no thunder could be heard, since the storm was too far away) during a freakish storm.

I have observed the Lightningflash energy occurring in two different patterns on the Circle: East-South-North-West and East-West-South-North. In each case the energy jumps across the center point rather than following its usual pattern around the circumference of the circle. The Lightningflash is also found flashing its way from side to side as it travels down the middle pillar of the Qabalistic Tree of Life. My experience of this particular energy flow pattern has been that it is a dramatic, intense shortcut, a leap that takes one beyond, or by a different path to, the next, sometimes unexpected, step. To experience it at work in one's life is surprising, frequently painful, but always for the best—since it frequently results in a dramatic, unexpected, spiritual growth spurt. Frequently, the gods gift us with inspiration and spiritual wisdom in the form of a *bolt* of inspiration, a *lightningflash* of knowing, the deeper meaning of which we then spend several years (if not the rest of our lives!) figuring out. I will speak more of the Lightningflash movement in later chapters.

EXPANSION AND CONTRACTION

The two primary forces at work in all energy movements are expansion and contraction. Expansion moves outward. Beginning as an inner, chaotic movement that is out of harmony with its local surroundings, the movement of expansion pushes outward, ultimately leading to something new. Contraction is the force that pulls things back in again. It is a hardening, rigidifying, densifying force. Together these two forces create, destroy, and re-create the world, endlessly; their action may be seen in the Elements, in the seasons, and in our lives.

THE WESTERN MYSTERY TRADITION

In this book you will find repeated reference to the Western Mystery Tradition, so perhaps some clarification is in order for those of you unfamiliar with this term. The Western Mystery Tradition (which is also known as the Western Esoteric Tradition and the Western Magical Tradition) is a term used for the esoteric spiritual traditions of the West. These include many spiritual paths—Greek, Egyptian, Celtic (which is where Druidry and Witchcraft come in) and Qabala among them. These spiritual traditions had an esoteric inner side to them as well as their well known, more public, exoteric aspect; the word "Mystery" was used when referring to the inner teachings reserved for the initiates. The esoteric aspects of these traditions caused them to be referred to as "Mystery Religions." The word Western is used to differentiate it from the Eastern Traditions of such places as China, Japan, India, and Tibet. (There is also evidence that links many Celtic beliefs, practices, and values with those of India.)

I can hear the scholarly purists among you crying out that since Egypt is in Africa and the Qabala originated in the Mideast, neither of them is "Western," that is, if we are defining "Western" to mean "European" as is sometimes done. My designation of them as "Western" is due to the fact that 1) as mentioned above, they are not from Asia/the Far East and 2) have served as foundation for the development of many magical systems of the Western Tradition, and 3) much of what constitutes what we refer to as the "Western" Mystery Tradition springs from an area better described as "Mediterranean." Qabalistic and Egyptian material was more readily available in Europe during times of magical development than was the equivalent material of the European native spiritual traditions, which had been downgraded to "primitive and barbarian" status by an officialdom impressed and imprinted with a Greco-Roman-Mediterranean mentality/worldview. It is heartening that, in the last few decades, we are seeing the re-emergence of many of the native European traditions, especially the Northern (Teutonic/Celtic/Baltic/FinoUgaric/Russian, etc.) and Central European (Bulgarian/etc.).

This is not a book about the Celtic Tradition, though you will find references to it scattered throughout. This book is rooted in the Western Mystery Tradition, particularly Witchcraft in its Celto-Germanic form, since this particular teaching has formed the largest component of my own spiritual path and study for over 20 years.

THE RULES OF THE MAGUS

Most of us practicing the magical arts have, from time to time, come across a magical motto known as the Magician's Maxim, or Rules of the Magus: "To know, to will, to dare, to keep silent." I remember learning these lines many years ago as part of my early training. Interestingly, these lines turn up in a variety of sequences in different magical sources. I have seen this motto *as to know, to dare, to will, to*

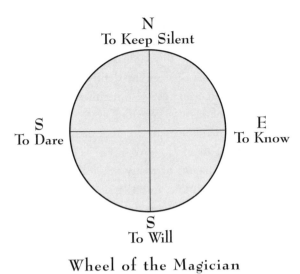

Wheel of the Magician

keep silent, but also *to will, to dare, to know, to keep silent,* as well as *to dare, to know, to will, to keep silent.* I have also noted with interest that the phrases have been ascribed to different quarters of the Circle, and thus different elements.

In this book I have chosen to ascribe knowing to the East, willing to the South, daring to the West, and silence to the North. Much thought on this subject, however, has caused me to stumble upon the truth that, in reality, each of these phrases can be meaningfully related to each of the Elements. Here are some thoughts on the various combinations.

To Know

We usually think of knowledge as having been acquired by the mind; it is certainly used by the mind. Therefore it seems appropriate that this phrase be accorded to the **East** with the Element of **Air.** Our English word *knowledge* is related to the Latin *gnoscere* and the Greek *gnosis,* both of which mean knowledge and are from the Greek root word *gignoskein* meaning "to know." Yet the dictionary definition of knowledge includes concepts of discernment, recognition, experience, and *practical* understanding—all of which seem more

related to **Earth** Element than Air. One generally "knows things" from having had practical, earthy experience of them. Elemental spirits of Earth are called *gnomes*—the knowers. So it is possible to see how *to know* can also be found in the **North.** Knowing involves perception: in order to recognize and discern one must first perceive, which frequently involves use of the physical senses. Usually the word perception is used in relation to the sense of sight, which cannot bring us information if light is not present. Sight seems to lead us back to the East again, but while light can be found in the East, South and West, it is most prominent in the **South**—time/place of the brightest light of the day/year (and therefore of the most direct perception), and ascribed the element of **Fire.** The light of the West is a fading light, it seems to go inward, just as we do to ponder and assimilate our experiences. Looked at from the **West/Water** perspective, *to know* means knowledge realized and deepened by inner reflection and process.

To Will

The roots of this word go back to the Latin *velle,* meaning "to wish, to desire" and relates to the act of making choices or decisions, to setting an intention. Hopefully choices, decisions, and intentions are based on knowledge (or at least information), and this shows us the **East/Air** aspect of *to will.* Intentions, choices, and decisions are movements toward manifestation. As such, they are representative of the principle of growth, which is found in the **South/Fire** position of the Wheel. Will implies a power of "push" similar to that of a growing plant pushing its way upward toward the sun—a persistence and toughness, arising from deep, inner instinct, in service of a goal. Yet wishes and desires, in the human realm, have a strongly emotional component, and this relates them to **West/Water.** The desire to see our choices/decisions all the way through to manifestation brings *will* around to the **North/Earth** part of the Wheel.

To Dare

To be daring is to be courageous, bold, and venturesome. Courage involves the feelings, and thus, the heart. The word courage itself comes from the Latin *cor* and Greek *kardia,* both meaning heart. We associate our emotions with the heart. Daring and courage involve facing, persevering, and withstanding fear and danger. It is scary to go into the dark of the unknown. To ride off into the sunset—**West/Water**—requires courage and daring, whether one is heading into the physical darkness of nightfall or the inner darkness of swirling emotion and desire. Though emotions are associated with the West, and the ebb and flow of the Water element, courage and heart can also be seen to be associated with the **South/Fire,** by virtue of the heat that emotions such as love, passion, hate, and anger can generate. To be daring and venturesome, one must exhibit a strength that is often more spiritual than physical, thus linking daring again with Fire and the South. To be venturesome one must be open to new ideas and new beginnings, thus bringing in the powers and qualities of the **East/Air.** And finally, it takes tenacity and persistence to carry through on a dare, and these qualities are linked to the **North/Earth.**

To Keep Silent

Silence is one of the qualities associated with the element of **North/Earth.** Magically speaking, and this will be detailed more in later chapters, to keep silent is to conserve/reserve rather than dissipate energies. To keep silent is to conserve strength and build power, which can also be associated with **South/Fire.** Yet it is also possible to see the power of **West/Water** here, since West is the Autumn/sunset place on the wheel, where night falls and its silent restfulness begins. It is the time of going into the silence: for rest, for visions, for dreams, for introspection. Silence is less understandable in the **East/Air** position, since this position is about coming out of the silence with the power of sound and light. As such, the best way to understand its relationship to East and Air is to think of it as the necessary balance. Silence is the balance to sound, rest is the balance to activity, introspection is the balance to seeing beyond the self, and inner vision/dream is the balance to outer vision.

PART ONE

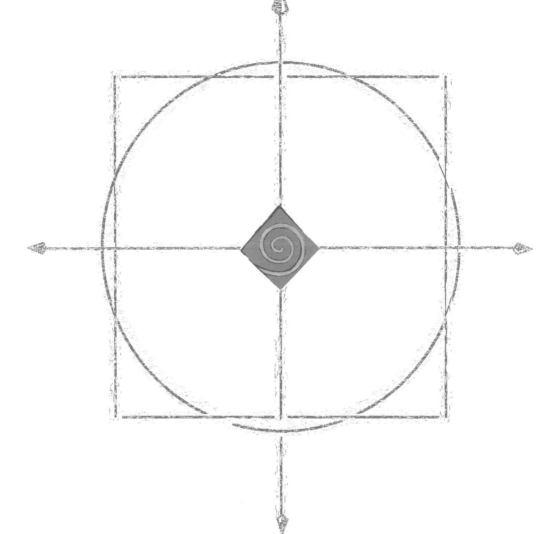

The Four Elements and
the Four Directions

CHAPTER ONE

About the Elements

In the beginning, there was, perhaps, some form of the "Big Bang," the scientific term used to explain what various ancient wisdom teachings refer to as the original movement within the Void of Potentialities, the origin of our universe. It is possible that we may, scientifically speaking, never know exactly what caused this movement (which physicists refer to as a "fluctuation within the Void"), as it may be apprehended by us only, for now at least, in a mystical sense. The "Bang," however you understand or perceive it, got the evolutionary ball rolling (in both a spiritual and physical sense); fast-forwarding vast numbers of years, we find gases swirling, spinning, and condensing themselves into stars, galaxies, and later still, planets.

Somehow, though, in this little corner of the galaxy, things worked out in such a fashion that what we call the Elements of Life (hydrogen, nitrogen, oxygen, helium, etc.) were present in just the right amounts for life to develop on a small planet circling a medium type and size star. Our ancestors, looking at the fact of our existence on this planet and explaining it in a slightly different way, determined that the "Elements of Life," the building blocks out of which all things on earth, including humans, were created, were the Four Elements of Earth, Air, Fire, and Water.

Though Empedocles, a Sicilian philosopher of the fifth century B.C., was the first (or at least the first we know about) to delineate the principle of the four elements as such, other philosophers contributed to and elaborated this principle with their own observations and reflections. Among these were the sixth century philosophers of the Pythagorean School at Samos (Italy) and the fourth century members of the Platonic Academy of Greece, who taught that there was a correspondence between the Elements and certain three-dimensional geometric shapes. These ancients believed in the underlying harmony of living things, and saw the universe to be a beautiful, orderly, and harmonious place. The concept of the "Platonic Solids," as these five geometric shapes came to be called, was part of the overall attempt of these philosophers to discover and understand the mathematical principles behind the harmony and order which they perceived to exist in both earth and sky. The Platonic solids are the basis for every three-dimensional form that exists in the physical world.

The Platonic Solids and their Elemental correspondences are as follows:

- Tetrahedron (which has four triangular faces) = Fire (4 triangles)
- Cube (which has six square faces) = Earth (6 squares)
- Octahedron (which has eight triangular faces) = Air (8 triangles)
- Eicosahedron (which has twenty triangular faces) = Water (20 triangles)
- Dodecahedron (which has twelve pentagonal faces) = Spirit (12 pentagons)

A FIFTH ELEMENT

Some ancient wisdom traditions teach of another, fifth element, though it is sometimes also looked upon as the first element. It is referred to as *Aether* (origin of the word "ethereal") and was thought of

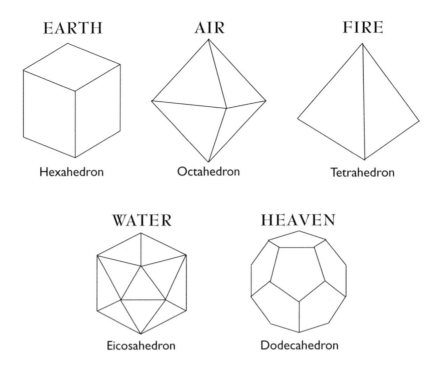

EARTH
Hexahedron

AIR
Octahedron

FIRE
Tetrahedron

WATER
Eicosahedron

HEAVEN
Dodecahedron

Platonic Solids

as a celestial, immaterial, rarified element filling the heavens and upper regions of space. It was sometimes referred to as Akasha, which means spirit, or *Pneuma* which means air/spirit. (*Aether* is Latin but from a similar Greek word; *Pneuma* is Greek and *Akasha* is Sanskrit.) Through the years this teaching (concerning akasha, aether, pneuma) degenerated into the conviction that the manifest, physical world (composed of the four elements) was somehow "unalive" until it was later "ensouled" or "enlivened" by this fifth "enlivening element" called *Aether/Akasha.*

This "separation mentality" perspective has always seemed disconnected to me, dividing creation into alive and not alive, as if some things are just *dead* until given life, in the form of souls or spirits—as if matter were *dead* and spirit was *alive,* and seldom, if ever, shall the twain meet.

One of the problems I see here is a confusion between the meanings of the words *soul* and *spirit,* which are frequently used interchangeably, though they do not really mean the same thing. In addition, the word *consciousness* (which has to do with awareness, especially *self*-awareness) is sometimes equated with Spirit, because Spirit is seen to be conscious, i.e., aware and self-aware. Also, I think there has been a misunderstanding of *Aether,* which I see to be a radiantly (*aithein,* the Greek root of this word, means to "ignite, to blaze") living, cosmic sea of being from which all forms become manifest.

The idea of the spiritual world as divine, and the physical world as devoid of spirit and thus separate from divinity is a very old one. It manifests in legends of the Fall from an original state of grace/union with God (be it humanity falling, as a result of the actions of Adam and Eve, or angelic falling, as a result of the angel Lucifer's rebellion against God and instigation of a war in heaven). But though we've heard these old legends for years, and been taught their meanings, still we must be careful in our interpretation of them. It seems to me that besides being interpreted as a fall from grace, they could also be interpreted as legends of the original movement (or harmonics of the original movement), the fluctuation from the Void, and thus can be seen to be stories of creation, of life expanding outward and manifesting into form.

The idea that matter is dead and inert till "ensouled" by Aether/Akasha is a curious one, that could be born only of a fragmented perspective that sees separations and fragments rather than wholeness; the trees perhaps, but not the forest. My own perspective tells me that since all is energy of one sort or another (of differing frequencies), then all is alive, all is spirit; sometimes in substance/form, sometimes not. All is conscious in its own way, though perhaps not always *self*-conscious; all is in *process*. The parts of the *process* look very different from each other. The part of the process where "conscious" spirit, by changing its vibratory frequency, manifests itself into physicality, looks different from the other end of the process wherein the physical vehicle "dies" and seems to become inanimate. The first part of this process might well appear to an observer to be an "enlivening" process, as if an inert, dead *something* were being brought to life, though few among us have ever seen this first part of the process (conception). More have seen the second part of it, where death brings the departure of the animating principle, the soul (and with it the personal consciousness), and thus a definite change in the physical vehicle's life processes, which then go into decline and ultimate disintegration. An understanding of the first part has most likely been extrapolated from observation of the second.

The truth is, as modern physics continues to push back the boundaries of matter and energy with the discovery of smaller and smaller particles, it becomes increasingly difficult to establish a clear boundary between matter and energy. Yet many of the discoveries of modern physics are simply providing modern explanations and jargon for what the great spiritual traditions have taught for millennia.

An interesting aside to this question of what's-alive-and-what's-dead is a recent news report that researchers have found living enzymes present in the bodies of thousands-of-years-old mummies. Certain enzymes (in this case found in both brain and bone tissue) were found to still be active at 20 percent of their normal (amounts found in living bodies) weight. Researchers said that the DNA proteins continue working until they are totally broken into atoms. (*Science broadcast, BBC Worldservice, January, 1996*)

The fact remains that life is composed of these Four Elements (not to be confused with elements as defined and used in the modern sciences of chemistry and physics) and one way or another, we deal with them on a daily basis. They are deserving of our conscious awareness of them, our love, honor, and respect. In the Craft we know this, and in our rites we honor them, call upon them, invoke them, and represent them in our temples and on our altars; the more presumptuous of us even try to command them.

I would like to suggest that it might be wise for us to regard the Elements as teachers, opening ourselves to what they may have to teach us if we approach them consciously and respectfully.

While reading this book, bear in mind that in different spiritual traditions the Elements have been assigned to different Directions. In my early days of study, this phenomena bothered me, till I began to see the geographic and philosophic reasons behind it; I began to realize that, indeed, there are as many different ways of perceiving, understanding, and trying to map out our world and life as there are people trying to do it.

In understanding variations of Elemental placement on the Wheel of the Directions, it is good to remember that spiritual traditions coming from geographies different than that giving rise to the Western Mystery Tradition have seen life's elements and realities in other ways (seeing different numbers of Elements and Directions), and thus have developed different patterns and seen different relationships in the same basics of life. For example, some traditions assign Water/Emotions to the South, the reason being that Summer, the time of greatest heat, can only be a time of growth in the presence of sufficient water. It is the relationship of water to growth being looked at here, rather than the relationship of heat to growth. Perhaps this assignment came from a place of scarce water, dependent upon summer showers. But this is a quite literal look at the Water/South assignation; perhaps it really sprang from an understanding of the necessity of movement and flow (Water) in the growth (Summer) process.

I have studied some of the other ways of assigning Elements to Directions and find them to be valid and sensible. The way presented in this book is the one in most popular usage by the Neo-Pagan community, so this is the one I offer to you.

SPIRIT MANIFEST

The Circle of the Elements used in the Western Mystery Tradition, of which Wicca is a part, positions Air in the East, Fire in the South, Water in the West, and Earth in the North. In many Traditions, the Center of the Circle is said to represent Akasha or Spirit. Spirit permeates all, so it is just as much the circumference and area of the Circle as it is the Center point. For magical purposes, I choose to view the Center of the Circle as representing Spirit Unmanifest, by which I mean the Great Mystery/Life Force (though perhaps it is more correct to say Spirit Manifesting), looking at the rest of the Sacred Circle itself as Spirit Manifest (Life Force manifested into form). *Spirit manifests itself into form through the agency of the Elements.*

I picture the center of the Circle as the *Origin Point,* the Seed. This is the place where the spinning begins; energies flow outward into manifestation from this center. The "seed of beginnings" divides itself (much as does a forming embryo) into *two* (the polarities), then into *four* manifestations. These four divisions are really four different movements of energy, the four basic ways energy moves and coalesces. Indeed, the Elements can be regarded as *processes,* as much as *manifestations.* These four "movements of energy" (frequencies or vibrations, if you will) are the Elements, through whose agency all else is formed. On my altar I have a special candle that I call the Presence Candle. This candle, sitting in the place of Spirit Unmanifest, represents the ever-present, variously manifesting Life Force (Spirit Manifesting), which flows forth constantly from this Center place in the Circle of the Elements. We are talking about movement, vibration, and process here, rather than anything static or frozen. The Presence Candle is, therefore, my representation of what I call the Cosmic Hearthfire, the Heart of Creation, the power of Manifestation ever emerging from the Void of Potentialities.

Obviously, the power of the Elements exists in the subtle, inner realms as well as in this outer one. (Please note that the Elemental teachings in this book refer to both inner and outer realms unless I specifically state otherwise.) What we refer to as our physical plane elements are but the manifestation, at our physical level of being, of these immense universal powers. But the physical form of the Elements with which we interact on a daily basis is *our path inward* toward contact with, and deeper understanding of, the Inner Plane Elements. By learning about and from the physical elements, we move toward a better understanding of these vast, subtle powers as they operate within the Inner realms.

In magical practice, when the Four Elements are referred to it is often that inner energy, that particular vibrational frequency, being referred to rather than the physical-plane manifestation of the Element. The *energies* of Air, Fire, Water, and Earth are the "forces behind the form," the energies that hold the template for the physical manifestation of the particular element.

Each of the Four Elements is a distinct energy, one of the four major building blocks of the Universe, if looked at through the eyes of the ancients, or through our own, magically trained vision. Each of them has certain unique characteristics that set them apart from each other, yet allow them to combine with each other (form relationships) and manifest as something different, contributing to the totality of energies and life forms on the planet. Each of them is unique, differing in motion and vibration, yet they are so interactive that to find them completely isolated from one another—at least in the physical realm—is a rarity. The reality is that they relate with one another ceaselessly. In addition, due to the holographic nature of life, all is contained within each part. Therefore, within each elemental sphere exists the whole Circle of the Elements. Paradox indeed!

This piece of ancient wisdom is illustrated for us by the Court Cards of all Tarot decks, where not only do the Swords, Wands, Cups, and Pentacles represent the elements of Air, Fire, Water, and Earth, but the King, Queen, Knight, and Page cards of each Suit also represent the elements of Fire, Water, Air, and Earth. Thus the King of Air represents Fire of Air, the Queen of Air represents Water of Air, the Knight of Air represents Air of Air, the Page of Air represents Earth of Air, and so on.

The Elemental Powers of Creation were considered so basic and sacred that the Celts swore oaths by them, using the Elements' truth and power as token for the truth and power of the oath being sworn. To break such a sacred oath was to turn the power of the elements against one and thus invite death. The Wiccan practice of concluding the first degree initiation oath with the words: "may my weapons turn against me if I break this, my solemn oath," is perhaps a modern rendition of this Celtic practice of swearing by the elements, the weapons in this case referring to one's magical,

elemental tools of sword/athame, cup, wand, and pentacle. According to magical tradition, the magical tools associated with each Direction/Element are the means by which the power of that Direction/Element is mediated in this world.

I'd like to suggest that as part of your process of working with each Element, you make (or acquire), ceremonially consecrate, and use the magical tool associated with that particular Element. This in and of itself will prove to be a powerful ritual.

No matter how you perceive them or categorize them, the Four Elements are not only the stuff of which we are made, but the stuff of which the whole world is made. They manifest around us, in their various combinations, in such a multiplicity of forms and energies, on all levels of life—physical, mental, spiritual, emotional—that their presence and power is an inescapable fact of our lives. And not only are they, quite literally, the *stuff* of which we and the whole world are made, they are, in their subtle form, the *energetic templates* for the stuff of which we and the whole world are made.

LIVING ELEMENTS

In spite of these many words (whose primary appeal is to the mind), it is always difficult for me to really explain how I experience these forces. Through the years, my understanding of the Elements has changed from a mental perspective of *seeing* and accepting them as physical, mental, emotional, and spiritual realities, to one of *feeling* them as Living Forces, as Spiritual Powers. I feel movement and power in them, and a certain level of what might be described as consciousness. Sometimes I am blessed with moments where my vision alters and I see the forces behind the physical forms of life, the forces that give shape to nature by interacting with each other—vibrant currents that flow through the land and interact with tree spirits, giving a certain form to a particular tree. I see land currents and plant spirits interacting with color forces flowing down from the sun that result in the colors of the various flowers. The reality of these blessed moments has altered my way of understanding nature, and the deep sense of seeing, sensing, and knowing I have experienced during such moments has given me a deep and utterly non-mental understanding of these forces and how they work.

It is my feeling that these other beings (nature spirits, devas, color forces, land and solar forces) work through the agency of the Four Elements. But remember, our human division of things into neat little categories is really only for the sake of mental convenience. The Four Elements are so interactive in the world and in our lives (by interacting not only with each other, but also with other forces comprising the larger reality which is Nature), and they are so much inside of us as well as outside of us, that I feel I must invite you to the feast of experiential riches that await you when you open yourself, if you have not already, to a world that is alive and of which you are part and parcel, not a separate entity, safely observing things from the outside.

I urge those of you who have not had similar experiences to go out into nature and make yourself available to the Forces there. They will teach you, and will be overjoyed that a human is demonstrating not only the willingness to learn, but the humility to admit there is something to be learned.

This book is rooted in the Western Mystery Tradition of which Wicca, Druidism, and Ceremonial Magic are major branches, but it also brings to bear the wisdoms of other traditions, particularly Native American Medicine Wheel teachings and elemental perspectives drawn from Traditional Chinese Medicine. There are many Ways in this wide world, and we are all humans, learning, experiencing, and sharing one planet. I, personally, have been drawn to study both of these subjects, but I include them here for other reasons besides my own particular interest in them.

I am an American. I was born on this North American continent, as were my parents. So even if a good percentage of my genetic heritage were not already what is considered "Native American" (Cherokee, in this case), I would still consider myself to be a native American. Many of you reading this book were also born on this continent, or now reside here. So although we feel connected to and feel led to practice the spiritual traditions of our European (or whatever land from which they came) ancestors, it is wise to remember *where we are right now.* We are connected to *this* land, this continent. We drink from its waters, its soil grows our foods, we breathe its air; at death it receives our remains, and then, we sleep within it. We are, quite literally, *of this land*—our physical beings are created from, and kept alive with its substance. In many cases, our roots here go back three, four, five generations or more, and the dust of our ancestors (who sleep within this land) also forms part of the substance of this land.

Admittedly, we are latecomers when compared to the indigenous occupants, but this *is* where we find ourselves at the moment.

With regard to our spiritual practice however, this does not mean we should appropriate Native American spiritual practices. It most especially does not mean that we are *entitled* to riffle our way through any or all of the special, private ceremonies held deeply sacred by Native Americans whose ancestors have been here a lot longer than ours, and whose ancient spiritual instructions tell them that they are the Keepers of the Land. We must learn to respect both the *spirit* of this land and the *Spirits* of this land, and that can only be done by tuning in to them and developing respectful relationships. It would be wise to learn about the traditions of this land—such as the Medicine Wheel—because we live here; we can be nourished by them at the same time as we are remembering the Stone Circles/Medicine Wheels of Europe,

Africa, and Asia. This is an Earth Wisdom teaching, and *we are all of the Earth*.

The same holds true with regard to Traditional Chinese Medicine's (hereafter referred to as TCM) elemental theory. This complex and precise body of knowledge also may be regarded as an Earth Wisdom Teaching relevant and useful to all humans. In point of fact, pre-Industrial Revolution Europe had its own version of an Elemental theory. You will find evidence of this theory in the writings of Hippocrates from fourth century B.C., of Hildegarde of Bingen (a twelfth century Benedictine nun, who was both visionary and mystic), and of Henry Cornelius Agrippa (a scholar, magician, and philosopher of the sixteenth century). You will find references to the *elements* and the *humors* (which means liquids) with regard to both physiological and psychological phenomena. The inspiration for this European tradition might have even come from the East long ago—there was certainly enough trade between East and West to have allowed ideas like this be passed back and forth. For whatever the reason, the European tradition was not nearly as well-developed as were the similar traditions of China (or the even older Ayurveda of India). Unfortunately, the European elemental tradition grew both rigid and degenerate with the passage of time, till its remnants were fairly easy to sweep away in the tide of the scientific revolution of the early industrial era. The remnants of the European tradition are definitely worth studying, but the Oriental and Indian ones are even more deserving of study because they have withstood the test of time.

The table below and the diagram on page 34 show correspondences according to the Traditional European Elemental Theory, developed over time by such great thinkers as Empedocles, Pythagoras,

Traditional European Elemental Correspondences

ELEMENT	AIR	FIRE	WATER	EARTH
Direction	East NE to SE	South SE to SW	West SW to NW	North NW to NE
Season of the Year	Spring	Summer	Winter	Autumn
Wind	Eurus	Notus	Zephyrus	Boreas
Name of Spirit	Sylphs	Salamanders	Undines	Gnomes
"Proper" Quality	moist	hot	cold	dry
"Mean" Quality	hot	dry	moist	cold
Characteristics	dark, thinness, motion	brightness, thinness, motion	darkness, thickness, motion	darkness, thickness, quietness
Temperament	sanguine	choleric	phlegmatic	melancholic
Disposition	cheerful, amiable	fierce, quick, angry	fearful, remiss, sluggish	slow, firm
Bodily Humor or Fluid	blood	choler or yellow bile	phlegm	black choler (melancholer) or black bile
Kinds of Bodies Compounded of	Plants	Animals	Metals	Stones
Soul Aspect	reason	understanding	imagination	the senses
Physical Sense	hearing	sight	smell & taste	feeling

Plato, Hippocrates, and many others. Much of this information can be found in Henry Cornelius Agrippa's *Three Books of Occult Philosophy*.

Thus the Element of Air is seen to be damp and hot; Fire is hot and dry; Earth is seen to partake of both cold and dry, and Water is seen to partake of cold and damp. Fire is said to be bright, thin, and have motion; Earth is said to be dark, thick, and quiet. Plato considers Fire and Earth to be "contraries." Air and Water partake of the characteristics of the other two, with each borrowing two characteristics from one element and one from the other. Thus Air is said to be dark, thin, and have motion (borrows darkness from Earth and thinness and motion from Fire), and Water is said to be dark, thick, and have motion (borrowing darkness and thickness from Earth and motion from Fire). Yet all is relative, so Air's darkness is not considered as deep as that of Water or Earth, and Fire is thought to be thinner than Air, and so on. Again, Agrippa's *Three Books of Occult Philosophy* provides more detail on this.

Each chapter of this book contains only a brief listing of elementally corresponding herbs and stones. There have been many wonderful books

written with lists and lists of these, and it would be pointless for me to repeat them here, much less to sort through the varying opinions. Plants have long been classified astrologically as being under the rulership of one or more of the planets. Consult some of the older herbals, such as Nicolas Culpepper's *Complete Herbal & English Physician,* for more information on this. But the way I recommend you handle this issue of correspondences with regard to herbs and stones is a way I have learned from my study of herbalism. I invite you to tune in to the herb or stone, to its energy as well as its appearance, and in the case of an herb, to its smell and taste. Try doing a bit of research on any herb you would like to use to see what the experts have to say about it. (Michael Tierra's *Planetary Herbology* is a good starting place; see Suggested Readings for others.) The decision is ultimately yours as to whether you feel aligned with what you have learned and/or intuited. Trust yourself, and be sensible. *Don't ingest poisonous herbs*—though they may be fine to use on your altar—just because your intuition tells you their energy is correct for your ceremony.

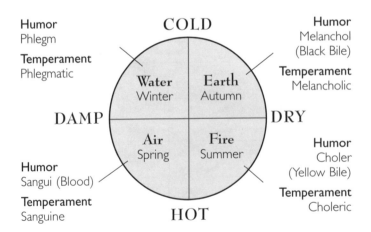

Traditional European Medicine Elemental Theory

A "Tuning In" Process to Contact

Done while sitting next to the plant or stone, or while holding them in one's hands. Begin with basic relaxation and induction. Set your intention that you wish to make contact with the essential energy, the spirit of the plant or stone you hold within your hand (or that sits nearby). Take the plant or stone in on a sensory level. Open your eyes and look at it, or visualize it in your mind, feel its texture, smell it, rub it with your fingers, and listen to the sound. If it is an edible plant, take a small taste of it. Then spend some time just being with and focusing attention on the plant or stone. Extend your aura out and your feeling capabilities with it. Even if you do not feel this happening, imagine it to be so. Imagine your "field" meeting and merging with the "field" of the plant or stone. Let this bring you information, and be open to the information it brings you. Once again, if at first you cannot "feel" this occurring, trust that it is and imagine it to be so. Be aware that this is a very subtle process, so be mindful of subtle feelings here. Note them; do not make an attempt to analyze, explain, or classify anything at this point. If you feel the plant or stone is opening itself to you, then you may proceed further. If not, it may be better to try this exercise at another time with another plant or stone. In any case, be sure to thank the plant or stone for participating in the interaction with you.

If you feel the plant or stone opening to you, ask that you be allowed further and deeper communication with it: ask that the spirit of the plant or stone communicate to you in some way. Do not hold any preconceived notions of how this will be. Just pray to the plant or stone, making this request reverently, and wait. If you have a specific reason (beyond idle curiosity) for wishing for this information (i.e., to help someone in need of healing by use of the plant/stone's spiritual healing properties), so much the better. State this reason as part of your prayer.

In working with stones I invite you to observe the structure, the shape and feel of the stone (to note its coloration), and also to tune in to the stone's energy. A bit of research in mineralogy books about the particular stone's formative process is also a good thing. For help with the tuning in process, try the exercise above.

ELEMENTS AND SEASONS

In the writing of this book I have followed the Direction/Season/Element correspondence that is adhered to within the Western Mystery Tradition—East/Spring/*Air,* South/Summer/*Fire,* West/Autumn/*Water,* and North/Winter/*Earth* (see Introduction, Wheel of Correspondences). All in all, this works well in magical practice. However, though a season is said to be "ruled" by a particular element, it is obvious to all that more than just that particular element manifests in any given season. To deepen our understanding of the Elements it is important to look at how they relate to each other during each season.

A season's energies and weather are a perfect example of the interactive nature of the Four Elements. In any given season, two of the Elements seem to predominate, with the other two playing lesser roles. Winter, for example, is traditionally ascribed to the rulership of the Earth Element; this quite aptly demonstrates Winter's slow, quiet, inner rest and regenerative qualities, as Earth's vital forces seem to be asleep during this time of year. Yet claim could be made that the Element of Water (in the form of rain, snow, and ice) also accurately characterizes this season, and obviously there is truth here too. Ice in particular, being water in "solid" form (solidity being an "earthy" quality), demonstrates the predominance of these two elements during this season. Air is present in the form of the damp, blustery winds which in this case carry the message of Winter's cold, wet nature. Fire plays an important but different role here. It is important to keep ourselves warm, to keep our inner fires tended, and to give honor to the fire of the newborn Sun at Winter Solstice, but Elemental Fire does not really characterize Winter in the same way that Elemental Earth and Water are seen to do. Rather, its role seems to be one of bringing balance to the extremes of the predominating Water/Earth combination.

Similarly, Springtime seems to brings the Elements of Air (movement and change) and Fire (creativity and growth) into prominence, with Water (introspection, feelings, fulfillment) and Earth (silence, age, wisdom, repose) playing lesser roles. To my way of thinking, Summer is most closely associated with the two Elements most honored as bringers of Earth's fertility: Fire and Water. The soil, well watered by winter rains and Spring/Summer showers, combined with longer hours of light and the hottest time of year, gives birth to the great profusion of the plant kingdom, upon which all animal life depends for food (and in the case of humans, shelter and clothing too!). Earth and Air play lesser roles in this season. But Element Earth comes into predominance with the time of harvest—Autumn—when Earth showers us with her bounty. Yet the Element of Water is prominent here too; Autumn's glorious burst of color evokes feelings within us, especially the bittersweet feel of Summer's end; as we store the nourishing harvest in preparation for Winter, we experience a sense of fulfillment and completion-of-cycle. In late Autumn the rains come, dissolving and cleansing away the remnants of Summer; Earth and all of nature prepares for Winter's rest and renewal.

So, although in the chapters on the Elements/Seasons I speak primarily of the Western Tradition's correspondences, please bear in mind the almost "dual rulership" aspect I have just described.

It is important to note that when working with the Elements/Directions in magical practice, traditionally a "Great Being" is invoked and called upon at each quarter of the magical circle. These four Great Beings are held to be the governing intelligences of that particular Direction/Element and are referred to as the Lords of the Watchtowers, the Guardians of East/South/West/North, the Four Holy Creatures, the Four Archangels, the Spirit Keepers, and many other names. These four Great Beings (under their various names and symbolism) are to be found almost everywhere that humans work with a system of Four Directions/Elements. These Beings serve as not only governing intelligences of their particular Direction/Element, but may also be thought of as Gateways or Gatekeepers into the particular realms of each Direction/Element. Though most frequently depicted in male imagery, they are androgynous. Therefore, they may be imagined not only as either male or female, but also as Beings combining both qualities, or perhaps as twins—one male, one female—standing on the right and left respectively, of either side of the Directional Gateway.

If you intend to go beyond the introductory level meditations included in each chapter and get further into "magical workings," it is wise to ritually call upon these Beings and do your intended work with their assistance. Likewise, it is appropriate to call upon them and acknowledge them when you are traveling in their realms. To these ends, I offer you a short meditation to be used in contacting these Elemental Beings (see "Journey to the Guardians of the Elements" in the Appendices). However, since this book is intended to help you reconnect with the Elements as they are present on all levels of your life rather than one that teaches you how to do advanced "elemental magic," you may not find it necessary to magically work with these Beings every time you are working with their Element, though good manners (applicable in any world you care to traverse) would demand that you greet and acknowledge these Beings as you begin your work with their Element/Direction.

This greeting and acknowledgment can be as brief or as lengthy as you desire. It goes without saying that it should also be heartfelt.

It is my hope that this book will be of assistance to you in understanding the Four Elements; that it will inspire you to experience them and to view your experiences in terms of them; that it will inspire your creativity in representing them on your altars and in your temples, deepening your relationship with each of these profound and powerful Elements. Toward these ends, I offer these pages of information, exercises, and meditations.

CHAPTER TWO

Earth

Although some people tend to mentally isolate each of the elements, and think of them each in a refined, purified form for magical purposes, there is nothing simple about the Element of Earth. It is a rich and beautifully complex element—being, as it is, the combination of them all. Earth is the manifestation through form, structure, weight, and density (i.e., substance) of various combinations of the other three elements. Earth is mountains, valleys, caves, beaches, farmland, meadows, forests. Earth is the wood we burn for our warm cooking fires, or use to build into our shelters; Earth is the food we eat, the teas we drink, the medicines we take, the clothes we wear. Earth is the plant kingdom, the animal kingdom, the human kingdom, but most of all—earthiest of all, densest of all—the mineral kingdom. In short, the Element of Earth is about substance and structure.

WESTERN MYSTERY TRADITION AND THE EARTH ELEMENT

Many of our European ancestors regarded the time period we call a day as beginning at twilight/sunset, so we will begin our study of the Elements and Directions with the direction of night—the North—and with the Element of Earth. Since we will be viewing the Four Elements in the context of the Four Directions in these chapters, we will start with a review of some information about the Direction associated with Earth. In the Western Mystery Tradition of which Wicca is a part, Earth is assigned to the Direction of North, the Northern Quarter of the Circle of the Year.

DIRECTION—NORTH

The North is the place of Winter, and of what is called in esoteric literature, the Midnight Sun. Because the sun never reaches North in the sky, North is the Direction of Mystery, of the unseen. The North Star is the Axis around which revolve the stars of the night sky. Altars generally face North in the Craft; sometimes they are placed in the North. The colors of North are the black of the Void; the black, brown and red of the soil; the browns, greens and russets of vegetation; and the white of winter snow.

North brings us the power to be silent (see the Magician's Wheel, page 22), to listen as well as to speak, to keep secrets, and to know what *not* to say. It is the direction of the Crone, the Old Wise One, who has seen it all, knows it all: the Goddess in her dark aspect. It is the direction of Death and Repose, the necessary rest that must come before the rebirth of Spring. As such it is the direction also of the various deities of the Underworld both masculine and feminine.

Since the element assigned to the North is Earth, the North is the place of the physical realm. Refer to the Table of Elemental Correspondences (page 18) to see a more detailed list of these correspondences.

As East is the place of the sunrise and West is the place of the sunset, so North is the place of midnight—literally the middle of the night, the time of deepest darkness and most profound silence. Yet North is also the place of the Midnight Sun, since it is at the year's Midnight, the point of Winter Solstice when the light of the sun is reborn. "From the darkness is born the light," we say in our Yule ritual. Our survival of the dark, cold time of Winter is dependent upon the resources we have prepared throughout the Spring, Summer, and Autumn to sustain us through this time. "To see the Sun at Midnight" (a very old, metaphysical concept) is to experience, while still in physical form, the mysteries that lie beyond the gate of death, thus coming to a personal, inner knowing of the realities of spirit. In the ancient spiritual traditions, this particular initiation was only embarked upon by those who had undergone much preparation and training, analogous to the above mentioned Spring-Summer-Autumn preparation of resources in order to survive the Winter.

To see the Sun at Midnight is to realize that from the heart of the darkness (death) is born the light (life). It is to realize that in the deepest of darkness shines an inner light, and that, by extension, the most dense and solid of all the realms, the physical plane, is suffused and permeated with the light/presence of Spirit.

This is very akin to the concept of the "stars within the earth," another very old concept which reminds us that deep within the darkness of the earth shines the "earth light," reminding us that earthly substance is one with the substance of the stars: we are all made from stardust, and that the light of spirit shines in the heart of matter. The North is the place of these great mysteries.

"From the darkness is born the light" is true in more ways than one, we realize, as we travel the Wheel of Life with its many days and nights, births and death, beginnings and endings, manifesting throughout the many areas of our life and beingness. At length, what we come to in our lives is "the light born from the darkness," a wisdom born of experience and the insight it brings; a glowing awareness of our own True Self and Beingness, in the midst of all the False Selves clamoring for recognition. Wisdom is the distillation of our experiences. After we have boiled and brewed ourselves up in the Cauldron of Life, wisdom is the resulting quintessence of all our experiences, reduced to a few magically potent drops.

Key words for this direction are silence, mystery, wisdom, darkness, cold, death, repose, peace, rest, solidity, and patience. Other correspondences associated with the Earth Element are structure, form, the physical body (along with its sustenance and growth), the earth (and her fertility), sensation and sensuality, strength, density, groundedness.

The Elemental energies are powerful, and as previously mentioned, each Element has a powerful Being whose function is to mediate the power of the Element for maximum benefit and minimum damage. These beings have been referred to by various names throughout the world (see the Appendices for names of these Beings in other spiritual traditions). In the Craft we know them as the Guardians of the Watchtowers, or simply the Guardians. In magic they are referred to as the Archangels, and in certain Native American traditions they are referred to as the Spirit Keepers of the Directions. These beings are often thought of as defined, distinct, and individualized Governing Intelligences who have evolved (or have been brought into being) for the purpose of controlling and safely mediating the raw Elemental power. Again, it is always wise, when working with an Element, to journey to meet its Guardian Being and form a good working relationship with this Being, no matter how you envision its appearance. I envision them to be large, glowing, androgynous Beings, often prominently displaying the magical, Elemental tool they use to perform their function of controlling and mediating the particular power of the Element. But I try not to be too distinct and defined in my mental imagery, as I find that sometimes this interferes with what the energy itself wishes to show me.

MAGICAL TOOL—PENTACLE

The magical tool associated with the North is the pentacle, the major traditional symbol of the Craft, a five-pointed star drawn or engraved upon a round surface or disc. Also used sometimes as symbols of the North are mirrors and shields; mirrors, not only for their relative roundness similar to that of the earth, but also for their ability to give us a clear reflection of ourselves (as does Earth life), and shields as a physical manifestation of who we are and what we have learned on our life journey (very similar to a mirror if you think about it!). All of these Earth Element tools are really symbolic of the foundational aspect of Earth herself, as the stage and setting, if you will, upon which and within which, our personal life drama unfolds itself. In a sense, any surface can be seen as a magical tool of the North/Earth.

As mentioned above, a pentacle is a circular disc upon which a five-pointed star, called a pentagram, has been drawn or engraved. Therefore, a pentacle is simply a five-pointed star enclosed within a circle, a figure which has found its way into widespread usage in art and jewelry, as well as the magical arts. I would like to go a little more deeply into this Earth Element symbol that has been so misunderstood, since the pentagram part of it seems to have become the subject of so much controversy.

The pentagram, or five-pointed star, is symbolic of the Four Elements plus the "Element" of akasha or spirit. When the point is upward it is considered that the Four Elements are crowned by, or in the service of, spirit. So it would then *seem* that when the point is downward, the Four Elements would be seen to be *not* in the service of spirit, but, instead in the service of matter, or materialism, causing the downward pointing pentagram to be seen by some as a symbol of badness rather than goodness. For this reason, it has even been adopted by Satanists and other "bad guys" as their symbol. This is a rather convoluted piece of reasoning which I will attempt to unravel here.

Pentagrams

A downward pointed pentagram does indeed point down to the earth: sky is up, earth is down. If, however, you are steeped, as is the prevailing culture, in Judeo-Christian ideology which says that 1) God, who is *masculine*, lives in his *heaven* and heaven is *upward*, therefore associated with the *sky*, and that 2) Earth, and by extension *all physical "matter"* (and frequently referred to as *feminine*), is *downward* (literally beneath our feet), the opposite of upward, and therefore must be associated with the *opposite* of God. God's opposite, in this ideology, is the Devil, said to live in Hell, a place traditionally considered to be located "downward." It then follows logically that a downward pointing pentagram would indeed seem to be a bad thing, symbolic of the power of the Four Elements in the service of that incredibly busy guy, Satan, God's eternal adversary. Further, this would imply that whatever is beneath our feet (down) is somehow inherently bad, and whatever is above us (up) is inherently good. Equating "matter" (which derives from the Latin *mater*, meaning *mother*) with "materialism" also confuses the issue, since "materialism" (although it also derives from *mater*) is a word with bad connotations, implying as it does, a purely earthbound, greedy, atheistic form of thinking.

If you refuse to accept this dualistic way of thinking, however, and refuse to regard matter—everything earthy, underfoot, and feminine—as bad, then the downward direction of such a pentagram just represents the energy flowing in another direction, not necessarily a bad one. It represents the powers of the Four Elements directed toward, and in the service of, the Earth. The symbol of the

Second Degree in Gardnerian Witchcraft is a downward pointing pentagram. To me it seems obvious that, since the Second Degree Initiation confers the power of High Priest or Priestesshood on a person, and such a power always entails service to one's fellow beings, this symbol is, therefore, a perfect representation of the powers inherent in that degree of Gardnerian Witchcraft.

So a pentagram, whether the point is upward or downward, represents the Four Elements individually, and the point (direction) through which they express or manifest their combined energies. From this perspective you can see how the pentagram, especially when bounded by a circle (becoming a pentacle), is representative of the physical, Earth realm—which is composed of those forces of vibration possessing the varying degrees (levels) of density and speed of motion that we refer to as the Four Elements.

Please note that, given the general level of ignorance and the limited thinking of many segments of the population, it is probably not terribly wise to be seen walking around even the most liberal and politically correct communities wearing a downward pointing pentagram. To do so is to court, at the least, misunderstanding.

ELEMENTAL BEING—GNOME

Elementals of this Direction and of the Element of Earth (which is regarded magically as a passive Element) are the *Gnomes*. The word *gnome* is derived from the Greek words *gnome* meaning "to know" and *gnomon* meaning "interpreter," and is related to *gnosis* meaning "knowledge." The Earth-dwelling gnomes are *the knowers*, implying that true knowledge is Earth-based. Everyone seems to know about gnomes, whether or not they have ever heard of sylphs, salamanders, and undines. Throughout the ages there have been many sightings of, and tales about, gnomes. Gnomes are always depicted as little people ranging from tiny to just fairly small, gnarled in appearance, and

dressed in quaint, old-fashioned costumes with pointed, frequently red, caps. It is important to remember that these beings are *energies,* and to remain open to whatever form they may choose to assume. Throughout folklore they are always associated with under-the-earth related work of some kind, such as mining for crystals and precious metals and gems.

I am reminded of the Seven Dwarfs of Snow White fame, and wonder if they were really gnomes. Some spiritual traditions teach that gnomes are male, and that there are no female gnomes. This is interesting, in that it would seem to be assigning male gender to the inner level of the Earth element. Since our Earth is generally referred to as *Mother* Earth, this would seem to be indicating balance of polarities: female outer, male inner. In certain Native American traditions it is taught that Mother Earth's molten inner core is part of Grandfather Sun, another way of showing the balanced polarity of life's energies. It is an old esoteric teaching that our current, physical self manifests only one half of our wholeness, and that the unmanifest part, our Higher Self, is of the opposite gender.

Some schools of metaphysical thought teach that the Elemental spirits we refer to as gnomes are not so much individual beings as simply dense *energies*, vibrating slowly as befits the most dense of the elements. This way of looking at them might seem to remove any aspects of consciousness or awareness; yet, to my understanding, this is not necessarily the case. Personal experience should be the guiding light here, though the old legends and stories are helpful too. The old stories are full of so many different kinds of nonhuman beings that sometimes it is hard for us, being far removed from the origin of the stories, to distinguish between them.

I am reminded here of other Earth Spirits, Devas, and Nature Spirits, and feel that we are dealing with a whole family of Earth Spirits, who have differing jobs or functions with regard to the

Earth plane. The nature spirits are, perhaps, helpers to individual plants, the devas to individual species of plants, and gnomes the helpers in the mineral realm, which is the "Earth of the Earth" realm.

I would like, for the purposes of this chapter, to emphasize gnomes (rather than devas or nature spirits), as representative beings of the Earth Element, because "Earth of the Earth" seems to get at an essential earthiness I think is worth exploring, that is, the aspects of solidity and physical substance. What is more solidly Earth than a stone— be it a plain, muddy-colored rock or a hard, sparkling diamond or crystal? Many legends about gnomes refer to their relationship with stones and crystals, depicting gnomes as hard and skillful workers, craftsmen working diligently and patiently to extract the beautiful stones and crystals from caves within the earth. Thus we can add to our understanding of gnomes the fact that craftsmanship, patience, diligence, and hard work are associated with them, all good, Earth Element qualities. Old magical tradition has it that gnomes guard the treasures of the earth. By this we can understand that they are the forces which work to maintain the very physical substance and structure of the earth.

STONES, CRYSTALS, AND BONES

In the same way that we use gnomes as the representative Elemental Beings of the Earth element, I would like to emphasize stones (rather than trees or plants), as representative of the physical aspect of the very physical Earth element. Stones are also Earth of Earth: dense, slowly vibrating beings, composed of minerals.

Humans have a long history of association with stones and crystals, and this association covers everything from mundane uses to magical uses. One has only to think of stones ringing a fire pit, the stone tools of our early ancestors, stones piled into cairns or built up into stiles, small stones

placed around medicine wheels, and the large standing stones megaliths found in many parts of the world, to realize this fact. The soil of Mother Earth is itself composed of rocks crushed through eons of time and weather into fine particles, enlivened by microscopic life forms.

Stones appear inert, dead—they do not move on their own, speak, breathe or appear to respond to stimuli in any way. Yet they do indeed have a certain, slow vibration, and crystals have long been and are still used for shamanic and healing work in many parts of the world by many cultures. Think of magicians and gypsies with their crystal balls. Stones and crystals were used for foretelling the future, channeling energy, and a variety of other uses.

In our personal physical realm, that of our physical bodies, Earth of Earth is represented by our bones, the most dense, solid part of us. Like stone structures erected by ancient cultures, our bones survive us. But though they give shape to our form, our bones, with their blood cell network and marrow producing interiors, are not as solid as stones (nor as solid as most of us were led to believe in high school biology class thirty years ago), thus illustrating the interdependence not only of all aspects of our physical structure, but the interrelationship of the Elements as well. Still, bones and stones are similar in many ways, often analogous to each other. "I know it in my bones" and "I can feel it in my bones" are both statements that convey a quality of deep memory and knowing, similar to that of a crystal's power to record and store information. Stones are the bones of the earth.

The solid-yet-not-solid example of bones is a good one for the entire Earth Element. The biggest open secret about the Earth Element is that its relative solidity, fixedness, density, and immutability is just that: relative. It *appears* to be solid, dense, and stable, but this is only by comparison to the other three Elements. In reality, the Earth Element is actually quite malleable, or formative, able to be formed. This malleability exists right along with the apparent solidity and fixity, just as our bones are relatively solid and dense, yet able to mend when broken. Our bones give shape to our form, supporting us as they oppose gravity. They allow us to stand upright. They have a certain permanence to them. Yet our strong, solid, and living bones are, in truth, webbed with blood vessels—rivers of nutrients—and connected with flexible muscles. The deep interior of many of our seemingly solid bones is filled with a substance called marrow, the ocean of origin for the substance of our iron-rich, red blood cells.

This core of blood-producing marrow might be compared to the streams of molten, mineral-rich magma within the body of earth, which, through millions of years of geologic process, work their way upward towards the Earth's surface, eventually becoming what we refer to as igneous rock (from the Latin *ignus*, meaning fire). Quartz-containing granite is an example of this kind of rock. The seemingly solid bodies of rocks contain within them flecks and traces of the mineral rivers of nutrients that gave rise to them, evidence of the marrow sea that gave them birth. In some ways then, rocks are like very old bones, hardened, compact, their inner structure honeycombed with mineral particles from their molten, mineral-rich, magma sea of origin, just as living bones are honeycombed with strong, connective, collagen fibers or filled with blood-producing marrow. The bone/stone analogy is far from exact, and I don't really wish to push it any further. But it is intriguing, none the less. Bone structure also bears similarities to the inner structure of a tree trunk, with its vertical, nutrient carrying columns.

Earth Element is solid, hard, fixed, and dense; yet malleable at the same time—an apparent contradiction. But it would have to be so (solid yet malleable), since the ability to manifest realities through the agency of the Elements requires a certain formative capability. Anyone who has ever fallen out of a tree or been in an auto accident, knows that Earth's relative solidity is pretty darn solid. Yet the very ability of our physical bodies to heal from such injuries shows proof of the physical aspect of Earth's malleability. Remember, this malleability is true on the Inner Planes as well as the Outer One. The implications of this are enormous: It means that our capability, and Earth's capability, for change and flexibility is more inherent than our society's previous, conditioned thinking has allowed. Speaking of change, consider the fact that our physical being, which we tend to think of as solid and permanent, is actually replaced regularly during a lifetime, due to the process of cell death and birth.

Malleability implies possibilities. In the Life process, there is really no such thing as complete rigidity. Because of the fact that energy *vibrates*—is in motion—and because all is composed of energy, any organism approaching rigidity will of necessity break apart in some way, so that motion may continue. Yes, Earth Element is solid, fixed, crystallized—but remember, *it's only relative!* Change *is* possible.

TRADITIONAL CHINESE MEDICINE AND THE EARTH ELEMENT

Interestingly, TCM teaches that the bones are under the rulership of the Water Element (rather than the Earth Element)—the Kidney Meridian. The kidneys in TCM are considered to be the storehouse of the body's essential, inborn energy, that with which we are endowed at conception, from our parents/ ancestors, sometimes called *ancestral chi*. In Western terms, this aspect of the Kidney Meridian energy is related to our *physical* adrenal glands, which sit atop our kidneys and whose secretions maintain correct salt balance; facilitate body growth, tissue repair, and sexual reproduction; and make kidney activities possible. In addition, they are concerned with the body's response to extreme stress, or, the famous "fight or flight" effect.

When I think of the Water Element I think of seawater, and thus of minerals; the minerals in seawater, saltiness (salt is a crystal), the minerals in seaweeds, and the fact that all life is said to have come out of the primordial soup of the sea. Our bodies need minerals in the diet, and many of these can be amply supplied by eating seaweeds (some of which contain a lot of calcium), so our bones can be nourished and strengthened by the foods of the Water Element. Certain studies, such as those mentioned in Susan Weed's *Menopausal Years*, indicate that osteoporosis, the bane of this modern era's elderly women, is probably more related to lack of bone flexibility than lack of bone mass/density. This fact again highlights the malleability and *relative* density of the Element of Earth.

TCM assigns Earth element rulership to the stomach and its task of digestion, and to the spleen, which, according to this system (which has different terminology and way of perception than our Western scientific model), extracts the vital energy from food. In Western terms, the spleen's function overlaps into what we would call pancreatic function, since the pancreas secretes digestive enzymes, as well as substances to help our body handle glucose and fatty acids.

Getting back to stones: There's something about a crystal's power of resonance and vibration that is similar to the electromagnetic quality of bones. Not being a scientist, I can't explain this scientifically; it's something I just "feel in my bones." Consider the following, though, and come to your own conclusions.

Some of the standing stones of Britain have been, over many years, tested by researchers involved in an interesting research project known as the Dragon Project, and found to be exhibiting a vibrational frequency pattern best described in layman's terminology as *singing*. They have also been found to have a high concentration of quartz crystal (silicon dioxide) in their makeup, making them into large energy-conducting devices with all the normal properties ascribed to crystal.

Tom Graves, in his *Needles of Stone Revisited*, compares them to acupuncture needles in the body

of the earth. The purpose of acupuncture needles in TCM is to have the physical device of the needle interface (by being inserted into the skin) with the nonphysical energy system that flows like rivers of energy throughout the body along pathways known as meridians, in order to remove energy blockages, and to cause physical changes to occur. Since this is so, it might not be too far out of line to assume that the standing stones and stone circles of the world, wherever we find them, might have had a similar function: to cause a realignment of the earth's energy system. It is likely this realignment may have been linked with the cosmic energies of the stars, since most of the standing stones seem to be aligned with the sun (at certain times of the year) or with stars or star groupings. Before there's a mad rush out to erect stones attempting to duplicate this ancestral feat, I'd like to remind you that such major messing about with the earth's energy system is no light matter. These early stone works were clearly erected by people who possessed a spiritual technology that is, at present, lost to us.

Bones have a high calcium content, but contain other minerals as well. And calcium cannot be assimilated without the presence of other minerals, one of which is silicon—one of the main components found in the singing quartz crystal of the standing stones of Britain.

Additionally, in TCM each element (and organ complex) has an associated sound, and singing is the sound of the Earth Element. The Earth Element is related to digestion, and singing is said to strengthen digestion and thus generally rejuvenate one's entire being (good digestion being the basis of good health).

How does this relate to us, to our earthiness, to our bones? Since it has been said that crystals and stones (silicon-containing) have the power to record, store, transmit, and amplify information and energy, then perhaps we know much more in our bones than our minds realize. Perhaps our bones contain much of our memory, perhaps they contain our more cosmic memories, or our original,

Chakra Correspondences

NO.	NAME	BODY REGION	ELEMENT	COLOR	ENDOCRINE LINK	ENERGY KEYWORDS
1	Root	Genital/Anal	Earth/Fire	Red	Gonads	connection to Earth, vitality
2	Sacral Plexus	Sacral nerves, Womb, Kidney, Bladder	Water	Orange	Peyer's Patches (Immune System)	creativity, seat of emotions
3	Solar Plexus	Solar Plexus, Navel	Fire/Air	Yellow	Adrenals, Pancreas	personal power, will
4	Heart	Heart, Lungs	Air/Earth/ Fire	Green	Thymus	compassion, love, connections
5	Throat	Collarbone, Throat, Jaw	Air/Aether	Blue	Thyroid	communication
6	Brow	Brow/center of brain	Aether	Violet	Pineal	inner vision, psychic talent higher intuition
7	Crown	Top of Head	Aether	White	Pituitary	connection to spirit

stellar, operating instructions; perhaps they act as some kind of a trigger point for information and memories stored in our cells. What ancestral memories do they, perhaps, carry? Do our bones, like stones, also sing? Have we forgotten how to listen? Maybe if we listen to what our bones tell us, giving them the minerals (many of which are found in seaweeds) they need to be healthy, thus restoring our primal, foundational relationship with Mother Ocean, we might remember how to live on the Earth in a balanced way.

Our bones are the part of us most likely to survive the ages. Many so-called primitive peoples have legends and beliefs about bones that have to do with renewal, regeneration, and return to life. It was the custom among the Northeastern Native Americans (maybe other tribes also) that the bones of bears and other animals killed for food must be treated with reverence, in some cases returned to the wild, so that these animals could come back to life again. Generally speaking, hunting societies knew and appreciated the value of life, aware of the intimate connection between life and death. Sometimes the bear's skull was saved and hung above the bed of the hunter who made the kill, or

perhaps above the bed of a medicine person, where it was said that the skull would whisper its wisdom to the person and provide assistance in other ways. Bones wrapped in an animal skin, in many parts of the world of our ancestors, were used ritually to aid in the resurrection of the animal. Survival through renewal is the theme here.

All of these things point to the theme of Earth Element in general, but especially *bones—Earth of Earth*, the most physical, dense parts within us— as the key to renewed life, resurrection, regeneration, true knowing and wisdom; the key, in other words, to True Life.

As above, so below; as without, so within. Stones, Bones; Bones, Stones. From Death comes Life, from Darkness comes Light. The eternal dance, the Yin and Yang, the complementarity, and even reconciliation, of opposites—all of this—is in our bones. This fact points to something else: renewed life, regeneration, and wisdom are all to be found *within* the density of matter— and *not within a separation from matter*. So those who seek enlightenment and renewal by attempting to free themselves of the bonds of the material world are, quite possibly, going at it backwards.

Another thing that must be said about the Earth Element refers to the body of the Mother Earth herself and the pathways of energy running through her, similar to the meridian pathways of energy that run through our human bodies. These energetic pathways of Earth have been referred to within this century as ley lines. But they are also referred to as *Dragon Paths*, harkening us back to the concept of the supposedly mythical beasts called dragons. Dragons have always been associated with planet Earth. In the Orient there are Dragons for each Element, but here in the West the association has been primarily with the Earth—the deep, chthonic, unknown, powerful energy that produces landforms and earthquakes, as well as birthing trees, plants, and rivers. I believe the Oriental model, that of Dragons associated with each of the Elements, but especially Earth, is a beautiful way to express the concept of earth's manifestation of all of the other Elements. In TCM there is a mineral substance, known as Dragon Bone (rich in calcium), which calms the spirit and acts on the Heart (Fire), Kidney (Water), and Liver (Wood which is Air + Earth) Meridians. You will notice that Dragon Bone (Earth) is herein seen to act on and thus balance the other Elements.

So, the body of Mother Earth has Dragon Paths through which her energies move and circulate, and so do our bodies. Think for a moment about the energetic resonance that must occur between Her body and our body, her Dragon Paths and our Dragon Paths. Could it possibly be that our thoughts and feelings—forms of energy to be sure, and intimately related to the flow of energy through our meridians by virtue of the particular emotion or thought being expressed—interact with similar ones within Mother Earth? Could it be that the work we do on ourselves, the healing of self-negating thoughts and emotions, actually feeds and heals Mother Earth similarly? It's something to think about.

CHAKRAS AND THE EARTH ELEMENT

The word "chakra" comes from a Sanskrit word meaning *wheel, disc,* or *vortex*. Our chakras are wheels of energy existing within our subtle, or nonphysical, body; spinning vortices that allow us to receive and transmit life energy, as well as to circulate it within us. Invisible to normal vision, the chakras are detectable by those who are sensitive to subtle energies. The chakras are points of intersection and interaction between the many planes of existence/energy. Those with clairvoyant vision inform us that each chakra displays a different color, telling us that each chakra runs on a different *frequency* of life's energy.

There are seven major or "master" chakras, and many minor ones. This book will not go deeply into this complex subject; consult Suggested Readings for titles that go deeper. However, since chakras have elemental correspondences, I have included a bit of basic chakra information in the table on page 46 and throughout the following chapters. What I have found interesting in my years of studying and working with chakras is the difference of opinion with regard to the elemental correspondences experts have assigned to each chakra. As with the elemental correspondences assigned to the Directions of the Circle/Medicine Wheel, I can see validity in all the opinions expressed; and I offer some of these opinions to you in the course of the book.

My personal viewpoint when working with a chakra is two-fold. As we stand erect in normal human posture, our feet touch the ground, and our head is toward the sky. Thus it would seem that the minor or secondary chakras in our feet and legs correspond to the Earth Element, and the Crown chakra at the top of the head corresponds to the Air Element (considering that we use our brains and minds to think and to process ideas, which are Air Element functions). The genital and lower abdominal body regions, containing the reproductive, kidney-bladder and waste elimination systems, could be seen to correspond to the Water Element, whereas the solar plexus and chest areas, which contain the cardiovascular system and major nervous systems connections, seem to correspond to the Fire Element.

This, I realize, is only a rough map of things. When I psychically tune into each of these sections, which is my other chakra method, things are not so cut and dried; I find the overlaps, the chakric and Elemental marriage points. The Earth is beneath, supporting, sustaining, and empowering all else. The image that comes to me of the womb/abdominal area is that of a cauldron steaming and simmering over a fire, seething with potential and possibilities. The cauldron, made of earthen substance (pots are metal, sometimes clay; in this instance the "clay" of our bodies) and containing liquid, represents both Earth and Water. Simmering, steaming, and seething does not happen without the presence of Fire beneath. So I begin to get a feel for the elemental "edges" of interaction; and I realize that the Fire and Water chakras in the middle body regions do not have tidy boundaries. I suspect that there are gender differences also: men tuning into the genital/abdominal area might feel a different balance of the Elements than I do.

When I tune into the solar plexus region, I find the feel of Water giving way to a fiery feel, actually, the feel of fiery Air, hot mist rising from the cauldron. This fiery, misty Air ascends upward, and feels very warm around the navel and the solar plexus itself. It continues ascending upward into the heart, where immediately I am aware of a much more distinct Air Element feel, mixing with the Fire. This feel of Air increases as my sensing process moves toward the Throat chakra region, and the ears and mouth. This makes sense, since these are the areas connected with sound and communication—Air Element functions. Tuning into the Brow and Crown chakras brings a feeling of

Air Element giving way to something even more rarified: the spiritual "Element" that is referred to as Aether, Spirit, or sometimes just as Space.

As you can see, the Elements, as met up with in the chakra system, refuse to stay categorized into neat, tidy, little compartments any more than they do anywhere else we encounter them! The chakra system provides yet another example of their interdependent and interactive natures.

I hope the information here and in subsequent chapters makes this subject something you wish to pursue in more depth.

EARTH CORRESPONDENCES

Colors associated with the Earth Element are what are commonly referred to as earthy colors (russet, citrine, black, brown, and green): the black-brown or red-brown color of the soil, the brown of tree trunks, the green hues of tree and plant foliage in their various stages of growth, the colors of the autumn leaves. In a wider sense, all colors found within nature (i.e., the colors of flowers, fruits, and stones) are Earth Element colors. I use these other colors as accents to the primary Earth colors.

Planets associated with the Earth Element (in addition to our own beloved Terra) are those that rule two of the "Earth signs" of the Zodiac: Venus because of her rulership of Taurus (and all things physical, beautiful, and sensual), and Saturn because of his rulership of Capricorn, which governs bones, stones, and other structures.

Herbs associated with the Earth Element are the Venus-ruled birch, daffodil, coltsfoot, daisy, elder, geranium, mallow, mint, motherwort, peach, pear, plantain, pennyroyal, plum, primrose, strawberry, tansy, vervain, violet, yarrow, and all members of the rose family which include apples, hawthorn, blackberry, and raspberry. Herbs that are specific healing for the parts of the body ruled by Venus and Saturn are usually associated with the Earth Element.

Stones associated with the Earth Element are obsidian, hematite, smoky quartz, and others traditionally associated with the first chakra energies of rooting and grounding.

EARTH PRACTICES

EARTH ALTARS

Creating Earth Element altars is one of my all-time favorite activities. There are several different categories of Earth altar:

Earth Element (pure and simple)

This is a simple altar, with brown/black altar cloth to represent the soil, or green to represent the grass; branch, twig or pine cone to represent the Tree people; some rocks or crystals to represent the Stone people; some flowers or herbs to represent the Plant people; a feather and/or small piece of leather or fur to represent the Bird and Animal people. A blue-green scarf may be laid across to represent a river, or bunched to represent the ocean or a lake. Sometimes we use antlers (instead of fur) to represent the Animal people (and also the Horned God). If you choose to use the cauldron, pentacle, incense, and candles on the altar, these can be situated, if possible, near the objects representing their element.

Earth (of a particular season)

This altar is similar to the above, but keyed to a particular season with the addition of seasonal items (i.e., spring or summer flowers, apples, berries, or whatever fruit is in season, Indian corn, pumpkins, evergreen branches, mistletoe, and a white scarf to represent snow).

Earth/Stone

This is one of my favorite ones. The altar cloth can be any of the basic Earth Element colors—brown, black, or green, though I think brown and black work better in this case. Rocks and stones may be laid around in circles to represent stone circles such as Stonehenge; crystals, of various colors, laid in patterns: circles, spirals, triangles, and pentagrams. If possible, a large bone, or representation of a skull makes a dramatically effective centerpiece to the Stone Altar. I try also to somehow represent the gnomes on this altar. Sometimes I use the tiny wool and felt gnomes belonging to my children.

But enough of this; I think you get the general idea. Let's go on to our Earth Element Meditation. It helps (but is not necessary) if you can read it, as well as the other meditations and visualizations contained in this book, into a tape recorder to play for yourself later on; thus allowing you to close your eyes and sink deeply into an altered state while you experience it.

EARTH ELEMENT MEDITATION

PREPARATION

For this meditation you will be baking Bone Biscuits, using Dragon Bone powder and Quartz water. Smudge a crystal with burning sage leaf, to purify it and remove undesirable vibrations, and place it in a jar of water for several hours. This will allow the crystal to charge the water. Look in the telephone book to find a store that sells Chinese herbs and buy a small amount of an herb called Dragon Bone (Os Draconis is its Latin name), preferably in powdered form. Os Draconis is the bone of very ancient mammals, mined in China. In TCM it is used to "calm the spirit"; to ease insomnia, a restless mind and restless spirit. Using the recipe listed in the Appendix, bake small bone-shaped biscuits, using Dragon Bone powder, and Quartz-charged water. These incorporate Earth of Earth into the biscuits in a dramatic way. If you cannot find Os Draconis powder, proceed using just the Quartz Water. (I must admit that it is the name of this substance, every bit as much as the medicinal properties, that appeals to me and seems to link it to the Earth Element.)

If you desire to do this meditation in ritual space, the area should be decorated in earth colors and motifs. Cloths of brown, black, dark green, and white are used for altar and for wall hangings. Some representation of a dragon should be present—perhaps a statue, pendant, or picture. Around the room are scattered crystals, rocks, flowers, branches, and other symbols of the earth, with rocks and crystals being the most prominent. Bones, if possible, should be used as part of the decor. Tarot cards from the suit of Pentacles may also be used, if desired. When all is in readiness, the ceremony may be begun by casting a circle, if desired.

INDUCTION

Get yourself comfortable. Close your eyes, take a deep breath, and relax. Continue to breathe slowly and deeply and feel yourself getting more and more relaxed and comfortable. With each breath you take in, feel yourself becoming more relaxed; with each breath you breathe out, feel yourself letting go of the cares and concerns of the day, breathing out what is no longer needed. Feel your body as you sit upon your chair or floor. As you breathe slowly and deeply, become aware of how your own energy feels.

Continue to breathe slowly as you allow your mind to calm itself and to grow clear and still. As you read or hear the words that follow, allow them to create images within your mind. Allow the images to become alive, full of light, color, sound, movement—all as indicated by the words of this guided meditation.

Enter into the pictures now formed and become part of the unfolding experience.

EARTH MEDITATION

You are standing outside in the sun, close to a mountainside; before you is the entrance to a cave. Pushing aside a few bushes, you enter the cave. It is dim and cool inside, compared to the warm sunshine outside. You walk inside it, deeper and deeper, and it grows narrower and darker as you go along. The walls of the cave feel rocky and bumpy beneath your fingertips. You feel rocks under your feet and go carefully to avoid tripping. It grows so dark that soon you are feeling your way along, yet you feel completely safe, surrounded by the Earth's darkness.

As you traverse deeper and deeper into the earth, you become aware of presences around you. You hear rustlings, and other footsteps, lighter and quicker than your own. You pause for a moment wondering about it, and listening. There are definitely other beings around you and they do not feel human; but you do not feel they mean you harm, so you continue your journey.

Gradually you become aware of another sound: a slow, deep rhythmic thumping. Like a heart beating. You wonder if, in the relative silence, you are hearing or sensing the sound of your own heart, but realize almost immediately that this sound is much slower than the human heart. The sound grows gradually louder as you progress and you feel the vibration of it. You feel your energy vibration change to match with this pulsating sound and know you are hearing, and feeling, the heartbeat of the Earth Mother. (PAUSE)

The narrow passage you are traveling gradually widens and widens again and you begin to notice a faint glowing light ahead of you. The passage twists, and suddenly it has widened into a chamber. As you stand there you become aware that this underground chamber is filled with a dim, faint, glowing light that seems to be radiating from its earthen walls. There are spots where the light seems brighter, and as you look closely at these spots you can see they are out-croppings of crystal that seem to magnify a light coming from within the earthen walls.

As you pause to marvel at the beauty of this crystal-studded chamber, you become aware of the feeling of being watched. It seems as if the cave walls have thousands of eyes that are most definitely aware of your presence. You allow yourself to extend your awareness in the direction of the watching eyes, and realize that you are most definitely not alone in this cave, but that there are many, many beings present; and that they are very aware of you. There are many different kinds of beings here, but it is the earth spirits known as gnomes that you feel most strongly, whose eyes you feel upon you. Greet them, and thank them for allowing you safe passage within their realm. Take a moment to feel into their energies and experience them. Feel your connectedness with them. (PAUSE) Now send them love and gratitude for the gift of their presence in your life.

You hear a noise, and turning to see what it is, you notice a crystal sliding down the rock-studded, earthen wall to land at your feet. You bend down to pick it up, realizing it is a gift from the gnomes. Take a moment to thank them for this gift. (PAUSE) And thank the crystal for coming to be with you. (PAUSE) You explore the crystal with your hands, noting the size, shape, feeling every facet, noticing the roughness, its smoothness. Even in the dim light you can see that it gleams with a faint color. Take careful note of all of these things, including the color, and know that they all are telling you things about this crystal being that the gnomes have gifted you with.

As you hold it in your hand you feel its vibration, and know it to be a living being, and it seems you can even hear sound coming from it. Pause for another moment now, and listen. (PAUSE) Reach into yourself, now, feel into your body, your physical substance, your muscles, blood, organs, and bones, into your cells. Find the place (or places) inside you that is stone. With the help of the crystal in your hands, feel this stone-ness that is inside of you—feel its firmness, its structure, its density, its form. Touch this part of yourself, go inside of it, merge with it, let there be no separation. Spend some time doing this. (PAUSE) Give thanks for the part within you that is stone.

And realize that the earth beings, the gnomes of structure, of density, of form, of physicality, also live within you, throughout your body, but most of all, in your most dense, solid parts—your bones. Send your love and gratitude to the gnomes for the many jobs they do and for the love they have for you.

As you continue to hold the crystal and feel its vibration, you become aware that, within your body, your bones have been awakened. As the crystal you are holding vibrates within your hand, you feel it in your bones, as they resonate with the frequency of the crystal's singing.

Your bones seem to sing within you, songs you had long since forgotten. You pause for a moment, to listen, but realize that this will take a deeper and longer listening than just the few moments you have now, and also will take a different kind of listening—a listening with your whole being. You know that you can journey inward again, to experience this, some other time.

As you feel the singing stone within yourself, reach out and pick up the bone-shaped biscuit that lies on a plate in front of you. Remember that in addition to the normal biscuit like ingredients, it contains Dragon Bone and water in which a quartz crystal has been soaked. Let this bone-biscuit represent all the stones/bones that are outside of you. Spend a moment blessing the bone-biscuit and thanking it. Now eat it. Receive it consciously into your body. Be aware of its taste, its texture, think about what is in it and how all of this has come from the Earth. Be aware that you are taking into yourself the Earth beings who live within this bone-biscuit, as you unite the outer stones/bones with your inner bones/stones.

Feel your union with Stone. You are stone. You are Earth. Be here now with this realization, solidly, deeply, in its fullness. Feel it in your bones as you travel the Dragon's Paths the energy takes as it moves within you and moves through the Earth, outside of you, and know that they are one. And realize that in that moving, and in that knowing, you are carried to the heart of the Great Mystery.

Continue to remain centered in this knowing, as you slowly allow yourself to become more aware of your surroundings. Allow your breathing to return to normal and when you are ready you may open your eyes, but do not speak for a few moments.

EARTH EXERCISES

1. Go outside and lie on your front or back lawn (or any available piece of earth). As you lie there, allow your breathing to become slow and even, and feel yourself becoming calm and peaceful. Become aware of what your body feels as you lie there: the feel of the grass or soil on your bare skin, or through your clothing, the relative warmth or coolness of the Earth beneath you. Allow your awareness to be completely in your body; do not attempt to think or judge. Just be aware as you experience the feel of the Earth, the textures of grass, gravel, soil, and the breeze on your face. Now allow yourself, body and mind, to simply merge with the Earth; picture yourself sinking effortlessly into a physical oneness with Her Body as you lie upon it. Notice whatever comes to you during this experience, but just notice, do not judge or explain. After a while, return yourself to a more normal consciousness by changing the rhythm of your breathing (take a deep breath). Begin moving your body a bit, stretching in a pleasurable way. Take three deep, full breaths with the intention of returning yourself completely to normal consciousness, then sit up, and when you feel ready, take pen and paper and record your experiences.

2. Using bones as part of fuel for a ceremonial fire was part of the Old Ways, something done by our British Isles ancestors. Why bones? Possibly more Earth of Earth, as well as offering the bone marrow, the vital blood-producing (Life's Blood) part of the bone, as a gift back to the Life Force represented by God and Goddess. Our ancestors may have not been able to describe bones or bone-marrow in modern scientific terms, but they knew enough to know that boiling them up in the soup broth to extract the marrow produced a strengthening, health building (life enhancing) broth. Thus they offered a gift of Life to the Authors of Life. I'm not suggesting you build a bone-fire, but giving bones a place of honor on your altar is a nice idea. Unless you are vegetarian, get some bones from the butcher shop and add them to your next pot of soup, being sure to boil the marrow from the bones. Be very aware, as you are using the bones either for your soup or on your altar, of the animal from which they have come. Say prayers to this animal, thanking it for giving away to you the gift of its life.

3. When you are in a very relaxed state, journey inward, inside your body, and into the marrow of your bones. Ask that you be given information regarding the state of health of your bones and marrow, as well as information regarding what you should do to improve that state of health. Express your appreciation to your bones and bone marrow, and journey outward again, returning to a normal state of consciousness.

4. Make a pot of soup. Make it thick, rich, and hearty. Unless you are a vegetarian, use meat. Use root vegetables—carrots, potatoes, onions, garlic, etc. Make the creation of this soup into a ritual. As you take your soup pot out of the cupboard, honor, bless, and thank the powers of Earth that created metal and the powers of the humans who mined it, smelted it, and shaped it into a pot. Honor, bless, and thank the Water as you put it into

the soup pot. Honor, bless, and thank the Fire as you turn on the burner under the pot. As you line them up on your cutting board, thank the animal and vegetables—creatures of Earth—that gave away their lives so that you could make this soup. As you cut up the ingredients, affirm with your full intention that you are making a soup to nourish and bless yourself and those who will consume it. Intend that you, conscious and aware, will partake of the gifts and wisdom offered by all the life forms present in your soup, and give thanks for this opportunity and these gifts. As the soup bubbles in the pot, honor, bless, and thank the powers of Air. Stir the soup, and be aware that you are bringing in the Air powers of movement to what is cooking here, and that you are alchemically blending the separate elements into a "togetherness" that creates something new. When the soup is finished cooking, serve and consume it with the same ceremonial intent.

5. Using ordinary stones, create a Stone Circle/Medicine Wheel to work with magically. If it is not possible to make it outdoors and large enough to work within, then carry a pouch with you containing smaller stones to create a "portable" wheel whenever and wherever necessary. Let there be enough stones for each month of the year, one for each quarter of the circle, and a stone to mark the center (this represents Great Mystery/The One). Or perhaps you would rather place two objects in the Center—one for God, one for Goddess. Carefully select each stone, and dedicate it to its position and purpose. If you are using the small version, use your creation of it each time as a meditation to align you with the powers it represents. Use it also for Full Moon and Elemental ceremonies. If you are using the

larger version, use it for any of your ceremonies, bearing in mind, of course, that stone remembers and holds energetic charges. See Suggested Readings for further details on Medicine Wheel construction and use.

6. Play with clay, and try to create a small (or large if you wish) clay piece that is appropriate for temporary or permanent use on your altar. As you work with the clay, realize that it is Earth, solid yet pliable, and when mixed with water, becomes more pliable. As you work the clay, let these thoughts lead you into contemplation on the nature of Earth, of water, of dry, of wet, of solid, of flow.

7. Plant an organic garden. Something small and manageable is advised; even just a few lettuces and mints would do. Don't take on anything bigger than you know you can really handle. Prepare the ground and do the planting in a conscious, ceremonial way. What you plant should be something useful—something that will contribute to your daily nourishment and well-being of body and soul. The discipline of tending your small garden will deepen your appreciation of the gifts of Earth.

8. Develop an awareness of and thankfulness toward the Element of Earth. Upon arising in the morning, when first you set foot upon the ground—take a moment to realize how Earth is your foundation. Practice the conscious and grateful reception of your food when you eat, consuming your food with awareness of not only how Earth has provided this food, but also of the alchemical transformation that food undergoes within us as it becomes part of our very substance. Get in the habit of noticing the beauty of nature as you walk or drive about during

your day (even if it is only grass growing up through cracks in a city sidewalk), and give thanks to the Powers of Earth for Beauty.

9. Get in the habit of going outside at night to greet the stars. The Moon and the stars are the Lights of the Night. The stars above are the siblings of our star, Sol, our Sun; so they are our relatives. Go out at night and greet them, love them, appreciate their beauty, draw in their light. Allow the vast expanse of the night sky to put the upsets of your life into perspective for you.

10. Compose an invocation to the Powers of the Earth Element. Work with what you have learned and discovered about the nature of this element and work at reducing it into a few relevant and personally meaningful words. Write it in poetic form if you like, or even in the form of a song or chant. Make it short and simple enough to be easily committed to memory, and let it reflect your personal feelings of appreciation and love for the Element.

11. Ask yourself the following questions:

• What things in my life are resting, dead, decaying/composting?

• Can I see/feel this clearly?

• Can I see how this part of the process makes way for and nourishes future growth?

• Are there elements of my life that need to die, so that I may move forward?

Seasonal Meditation: Sensing Winter

This guided Visualization was originally designed for children (as were the other seasonal visualizations throughout this book), but may be used by children of all ages. After you have done it for yourself, do it with your children!

This is an activity to help you connect with the powers that are flowing through nature at this time of the year—Winter. According to our calendar Winter stretches (in the Northern Hemisphere) from December 21, Winter Solstice, until March 21, Spring Equinox. This is the official astronomical timing of the Winter season—beginning on the shortest day and longest night of the year—though the Wiccan Wheel of the Year notes Samhain as the beginning of Winter. But how Winter manifests depends where you live. I live in coastal, central California where winters tend to be shorter and less severe than some other parts of the country, and the full impact of Winter frequently does not hit till early January and sometimes is gone by mid to late February (though last year the rains and cold weather continued on into May!). So please use this activity whenever it feels like the right time to do it.

This Visualization will of course vary depending on what winters are like in the area in which you live. There is a wide variety of winter weather. Please adapt this visualization to suit your locale. If you live in a place with severe winters, pick a winter day that is mild enough to be outside without undue risk, perhaps one with bright sunshine, yet snow on the ground. Or perhaps one with a gray, threatening sky, with the smell and feel of coming rain or snow. If you don't live in a place where it snows, pick a day that feels wintery, yet that you can be outside in with relative comfort.

Find a place in your backyard or in a nearby park where you can be alone and undisturbed for a while. This place should feel like a good place to you, it should call to you to come and be there. The place should be full of the wintery manifestations of your particular geographical area—snowy, damp with recent rain, with trees nearby, perhaps some of them bare of leaves, silhouettes seen against a pale winter sky.

When you have found your place, stand there for a few moments and settle yourself into it. Close your eyes and take a deep breath, then let it out slowly. Keep breathing slowly as you feel yourself calming down and your energy becoming the same as the energy of your location. Feel your aura (the energy field around your body) growing and expanding to touch all that is around you. Use your imagination to do this: Simply imagine a glowing field of light around your body that grows larger or smaller as you wish it to. Picture this in your mind.

In your mind, draw around yourself a golden circle of protective light and thank the God and Goddess for the privilege of being part of such a beautiful planet. Ask the Devas and Nature Spirits to come and be with you and help you appreciate the beauty and wonder of the Earth.

Now open your eyes and look around at everything. Look at the sky and clouds above you, the winter-covered earth beneath you, the dead or dormant plants and trees around you— perhaps there are evergreen trees in your area. Whatever there is, look at it all slowly and carefully, noticing the subtle winter colors; noticing the way the light touches everything and creates contrasts, the patterns of light and shadow. If there is snow, notice how it looks as it clings to the trees and lays upon the rooftops. If there has been rain, notice how the drops look as they drip from plants, trees, and surrounding buildings. Look at each thing separately and then at how it looks all together. Just look at it all and drink it into yourself, as if this beautiful winter scene were a nourishing drink for your soul—as indeed it is. Use your breath and breathe it all into you. Take time doing this, and when you are finished give thanks for the what you have seen, and give thanks for the gift of sight.

Focus now on your sense of smell. Begin sniffing, and noticing which smells and aromas are present. Can you smell the cold, dampness of the earth, the smell of layers of fallen, damp leaves? How do the plants and trees nearby smell, or can you detect an aroma at all? Or perhaps you live where the winters are not so damp; is it a drier, earthy smell you are noticing? If you are near the ocean can you smell the saltiness in the air? If you are near a stream or pond do you detect any scents from these places? Perhaps there is an aroma of wood smoke in the air from fireplaces or woodstoves? Now smell all of these fragrances together and breathe them into you, allowing them to flow through your whole body with the movement of your breath. Feel nourished by them. When you are finished, give thanks for what you have smelled, and give thanks for the gift of smell.

If you live in a snowy, relatively unpolluted place, reach down and take a small amount of snow into your hand. Close your eyes now and put the snow into your mouth, allowing it to melt before you swallow it. If it is raining, open your mouth and let some of the rain fall in. What does it taste like? Does it taste like just ordinary water, or is there another, more subtle flavor? If there are any edible plants still around, ask permission of one and pick off a leaf to taste. Realize that you are tasting winter, when most of the plant's life force has been pulled within the

plant and down to its roots; realize that the plant could taste quite different in the Spring. Chew and swallow this piece of plant, taking it into you as the holy thing that it is. Give thanks to the plant for sharing itself with you. Give thanks for what you have tasted, and give thanks for the gift of taste.

Now close your eyes again and listen to the sounds of Winter around you. Listen carefully to each and every sound. What do you hear? Do you hear rain or snow falling? The sound of people or animals walking on a damp or snowy ground? Is the wind blowing? Are there dogs barking? Are there birds chirping, people talking? Can you hear the wind in the trees or the sound of water flowing? Listen carefully to all the sounds around you. Then separate them out and listen to each sound separately; then listen to them all together again, as if they were an orchestra playing a symphony for you. Drink this into you, these sounds of Winter; breathe them in with the cold air as you breathe it in. Take your time doing this and when you are finished, give thanks for what you have heard and give thanks for the gift of hearing.

Lie down now upon the ground and begin to feel what is under and around you. First of all, feel yourself as you lie upon the ground. What does your body feel like now? Are you comfortable or not? Are you cold, or comfortably cozy in your winter warm clothes? How does the chill of Winter make you feel? Does it excite you, inspire you, or make you wish for Spring to come? Now feel the ground on which you are lying. Is it hard or soft beneath you, wet or dry? Does it feel smooth, grassy, muddy, snowy, bumpy, or rocky? What does the upper surface of your body, the side of you that is not in contact with the ground, feel like now? Is there a breeze blowing? Can you feel the warmth of the sun as it shines on you, or is the day just too cold, with the sun providing mostly brightness? Let your aura expand very much during this activity, reach out with your aura, using your imagination to do so, because reaching out with your aura will allow you to feel more. Reach out beneath you now with your aura, so that part of your aura is allowed to sink down into the earth and feel it. What does the Earth slightly below the surface feel like to you? What is her energy like now? Does it feel solid, heavy and slow, or light and flowing? (PAUSE) Or perhaps something totally different? (PAUSE) Feel the Earth energies as they sleep deep within, preparing themselves to surge upward again in the Spring. Reach your hands out now and connect with what is around you on the ground. Pick up a rock or twig, finger the stems of a plant, pick up some snow, or dip your finger into some mud. Let your fingers trace the roughness of a tree trunk or root. Allow yourself to feel this, with both your physical sense of touch and with your energy sensing abilities. Drink these sensations into you, breathe them in with your breath, and when you are finished give thanks for what you have felt and sensed, and give thanks for the gift of feeling.

Can you feel how you are part of everything you have seen, tasted, smelled, heard, touched and felt? You are indeed a part of it all, yet you are your own unique self, too.

Open your eyes now, as you lie upon the ground. Be aware of what all your senses are bringing to you. Look up at the sky, then all around. Taste the lingering taste of the whatever it is you have tasted, sniff the fragrances and aromas around you, listen to the sounds surrounding you, feel the Earth beneath you and the energies of the plants and nature spirits all around you. Feel the difference of this season of Mother Earth from the others.

Sit up and make yourself comfortable. Feel your own energy running inside of you and let it fountain forth from the top of your head and from your hands and feet, using your imagination and visualization powers to help you do this, if necessary. Feed this energy to the world around you. Share yourself with all that has shared itself with you. Once again, give thanks to the trees, the plants, the animals, the wind, the rain, the snow, and the sky. Give thanks also to the Nature Spirits and the God and Goddess. Tuck this experience safely inside you to remember forever, and bid the sights, smells, sounds and tastes of Winter farewell, with love and gratitude in your heart.

When you feel ready, get up and go home.

CHAPTER THREE

Air

All four of the Elements are truly "elements of life," basic elements necessary to the existence and continuation of life, because, quite literally we could not live without any of them. Quite obviously we could not live without the process of inspiration and expiration of Air—breathing! We breathe in and out of our bodies a tremendous quantity of air each day. As we breathe in and out, we move air in and out of our lungs; our lungs separate the oxygen from the other gases present and take it into our bloodstream where it travels throughout our bodies, nourishing us by oxygenation as it goes. We exhale the gases which we do not need. Our life as a separate, independent being begins (though we continue to need a Mother's care) when we draw our first breath: the Breath of Life. It is from this moment in time that one's astrological chart is calculated.

Another way to state this is to say that one of the qualities of the Element of Air is *Movement*. Air moves. We breathe in and out. Breezes and winds blow. Things are moved as a result of Air movement (wind), and changes occurs. Thus change is also a part of the nature of the Element of Air. The winds of change blow through us, through the world—bringing fresh air, fresh ideas, bringing the unexpected, changing the atmosphere, freeing things up, much as a leaf is loosened from its tree by the wind. Thus we see the transformative power of the Element of Air.

We cannot *see* the wind (though we can certainly *feel* it) as it blows through the trees, only the result of its blowing in the movement of the branches. Likewise, though we can *feel* thoughts and ideas in the form of the emotion and intuition they induce, we cannot *see* them as they move through our minds. Their only manifestation is in the action we undertake to bring our thoughts and ideas into being, our reply to the internal movement of inspiration.

The Element of Air carries thoughts and ideas, dreams and aspirations out of our minds and beyond us, as we speak them and manifest them, just as a breeze carries pollen, seeds, and spores through the air to land and begin new lives far from their plant-being of origin. The Element of Air allows us to move, to soar beyond our physical selves, to explore, to wander, and to wonder. When we speak our thoughts, we use air and vibration to put those thoughts out beyond the confines of our head. The vibration thus created (our own personal vibration as well as that of the thought or idea) goes forth from us: Self-Expression. There is power inherent in these vibrations, thus there is power in the spoken word. Thus Air *connects* us with what is outside of and beyond ourselves: the other.

It is interesting to note that the word "spirit" comes from the Latin *spiritus* meaning "breath," and is related to *spirare* meaning "to blow, breathe." The Latin *spiritus* is also root to other related words, such as inspiration, respiration, and aspiration. The movement of Spirit through the world was seen to be like that of Air/Wind. This movement was also noted in humans, particularly with regard to their minds—thoughts and ideas coming and going, carried outside of themselves by the vibration of sound/voice. Thus the spirit-mental aspect of ourselves allows us to not only move beyond our physical selves, but to connect with what is beyond us. Remembering that spirit pervades and permeates not only all the Elements, but also all aspects of Life, it is easy to see how it is Spirit that connects and relates all together in the Web of Life.

In these explanations, it may look as if the quality of Spirit belongs in the East with Air rather than the South with Fire where it is most generally assigned (though I feel that "soul" is a more appropriate expression of South/Fire, see *Chapter 4, The Element of Fire*), and there is definitely overlap occurring here. Spirit, in its active aspect, partakes of the nature of both Fire and Air: Breath of Life, Spark of Life. My way of viewing this is that Air must feed Fire if Fire is to burn. Expression of Spirit comes only when preceded by (and fed by) Air's unique moving and connecting qualities. Air is the medium that allows the spark to catch, flame forth, and burn brightly.

Speaking of Air as a *medium* brings to mind the viewpoint of the medieval magicians that Air was, in a sense, more of a medium than an Element proper. Henry Cornelius Agrippa taught that Air permeates all things, connecting and binding them together (almost like glue) as it moves through them, as well as having the ability to carry "influences" (what we would call vibrations) from Being to Being and body to body, thus acting as a medium of reception and exchange, as well as of joining.

It is possible to see here, once again, the close relationship between the Element of Air and Akasha/Aether/Spirit. This is so because Air, along with the other three elements, are particular *expressions* of Spirit, a fact perhaps easier to discern in the active modes of Air and Fire than the passive modes of Water and Earth. Spirit breathes and blazes, Spirit flows and abides.

An important Air/mental faculty which deserves to be mentioned here is *imagination*. Our imagination, or ability to create mental images, is one of our most valuable tools. We have been taught little respect for this marvelous gift; we have,

in fact, been taught to dishonor it: "It's only imaginary, it's all in his imagination." Yet imagination is the first step we take in the process of manifestation. If we cannot imagine something, we cannot create it, we cannot manifest it. Imagination is our structure-creating device for accessing subtle energies. In its highest use, it allows us to access the Gods and Goddesses, by creating a mental form or matrix for those subtle energies to flow through to us. This form is then empowered by the energies flowing through; the form seems to take on a life of its own, and the inner images we see act, move, and speak in ways that we have not pre-programmed (as anyone with experience in inner journeying can tell you).

Like any powerful tool, imagination can be used for good or ill. We daily encounter and deal with powerful mental images, created by others and intentionally projected toward us in the form of mass media entertainment and advertising. Witness the power that both advertising and entertainment (television, movies, plays, the written word) can hold over us, creating powerful images that cause emotions and desires to arise within us. We should never forget that images are very powerful and that the power of image-making can be used not only *by* us, but *against* us, for the purpose of manipulation. Those of us raising children should be especially mindful of this fact, and give consideration to the media images we allow to be implanted into their young, suggestible minds. The power of the imagination is such that we should treasure it, nourish it, strengthen it, and use it wisely.

WESTERN MYSTERY TRADITION AND THE AIR ELEMENT

DIRECTION—EAST

In the Western Mystery Tradition of which Wicca is a part, Air is assigned to the Eastern Quarter of the Circle. The East is the place of the very first light of the sun as it rises over the Eastern horizon, the time of the day referred to as Dawn. The light experienced at this time of day ranges from the dim, mild, first few rays of light through a growing brilliance, to the full, bright light of a new morning.

The East is the place of Springtime, of sunrise, and thus of new beginnings, birth and renewal. It is a time of germination and the beginning of growth, as evidenced by new plants sprouting up all around and trees beginning to leaf out. There is a particular shade of vibrant green seen in nature at this time of year; nature is bursting with new life and vitality. Many baby animals are born in the Spring. I am reminded of the baby bunnies and tiny chicks associated with the Easter celebration.

At the East the movement of the light and of Life's energy is *outward*, so the East is the place of the beginning of outer expressions of inner life. East is the "firstborn" from the Center. And what a beginning it is! The East is a place bustling and bursting with activity. It is a time when the winter dreams of Mother Earth come to life, manifesting as new growth of plants, trees, and baby animals. Creeks and streams silenced by the icy grip of Winter are unlocked by the warmth of the young Sun and now make their voices heard in the land, rushing and bubbling along within their banks. Tiny green shoots force their way through fertile soil as well as through cracks in the pavement. All of Life's energies are moving again, and it is with an outward, pushing, thrusting motion that they are moving. Life is quite literally springing forth all around, and thus we call it Springtime. The very word *spring* comes from an old German word meaning "to jump," which in its turn derives from a Greek word meaning "to hasten."

The East is known as the place of the Mystery of the Great Breath. In many old mystical traditions, the Cosmos is breathed into being on the Divine Exhalation, and out of being on the Divine Inhalation of the Great Creative Power. This Great Power (known in some Native American Traditions as the Zero, and as simply "God" to most of us) breathes in and out, expands and contracts, creates and destroys. As the Great Breath goes forth, its movement is a whirlwind, a spiral; thus the cosmos spirals and coils into material existence. Similarly, materiality will unwind and spiral back to into the Divine Essence, the Void, when the Great Breath is inhaled fully once more.

As the Great Breath spirals outward, its movement creates vibration, and thus sound. The Sound becomes Tone; the Tone becomes the Word. The spiraling continues, and the Word creates the world. The Tone has harmonics, overtones, and undertones, and thus the many worlds, each with its own song, come into being.

The origin of all is in the spiraling movement of the Great Breath, which creates what ancient philosophers and mystics referred to as the Music of the Universe: the combined vibrations/sounds of each unique piece of existence. Thus does the Zero, the Great Mystery, utter forth Creation on the power of the Great Breath.

The power of Air—vibration, sound, tone, music, the spoken word—to bring change on levels ranging from consciousness and emotional states, to the physical structures of the human body or the "walls of Jericho," should not be underestimated.

The East is the place of these great and wonderful mysteries.

Both Spring and dawn are times of awakening and beginning; the starting point of putting into execution plans previously made, plans that will lead to a future harvest. It is the time to begin working toward the Autumn harvest. It is *Planting Time*, yet also the *time of first growth* for those seeds planted by Mother Earth herself during the previous Autumn's seed-fall time.

Like the Autumn Equinox, the moment of Spring Equinox is a time of twilight (two-lights); it is neither light nor dark, day nor night, but a time when the world and life are poised, balanced between the two. In this case, the twilight moves toward dawn: the Spring Equinox is the Morning of the Solar Year.

The daylight hours are equal with the night hours at the Spring Equinox, and from this point onward the number of daylight hours will increase and the dark hours will decrease. The increasing light allows for ever clearer vision of the future toward which we proceed. We begin to stretch toward the new possibilities that beckon to us from the future. The East is the place of illumination and clarity.

The East is the place of the mind, the mental realms of ideas and thoughts, of learning and instruction. In addition to the quality of clarity about this direction, there is also a piercing quality, just as the clear, bright rays of sunlight pierce the night sky's darkness at the dawning of a new day. As the world lights up at sunrise, we can look around and *know* what is there. We perceive, and our minds immediately organize our perceptions into recognizable patterns. Therefore the East is, on the circle of the Magician's Wheel, the place of *knowing*.

MAGICAL TOOL—SWORD

The magical tool for the East is the sword (see Table of Elemental Correspondences, page 18). At this point, however, I must refer back to the previously mentioned difference of opinion as to whether the wand or the sword is representative of the South/Fire (or the East/Air). A case can be made for either tool being representative of the Air Element. However, I feel more comfortable using the sword (of which the athame is a smaller, more personal version) as the magical tool for the East, as the wielding and thrusting of it seems more associated with the quality of "light piercing through the darkness" associated with the direction of East than does wand-wielding. In popular mythology the sword is associated with various heroic types and is always associated with the masculine power of bringing about a dramatic change; the rising sun is seen by some to be its victory over the darkness of night. In Irish mythology the Sword of Nuada (king of the Tuatha De Danaan

or people of the Goddess Danu) is the Sword of Light. Actually, any form of blade with a hilt may be used as the tool of the East.

Summon to your mind a picture of yourself holding a sword. Picture yourself with this sharp, precise tool and notice how you can cut, thrust, parry, and pierce the area in front of you, and around you on both sides. Now visualize the rising sun, and take notice of how, as it arises, the darkness is turned to light; as the light illuminates all that is around it. This should help you see the analogy between the Power of the Sword and the energy of the bright light of mind/consciousness/knowingness/awakening as it pierces through the darkness of unconsciousness. Or, to put it more poetically, "as the magical Sword of the East pierces through the darkness of Confusion of Mind, we are brightened by the light of Self-Awareness."

An elongated cross shape is inherent in sword and hilt. The elongated cross, distinguished from the equal armed cross by the elongation of its vertical beam, brings to mind the Christian cross of crucifixion—to Christians, a symbol of Life gained through a death. The equal armed cross of the Four Directions/Seasons which represents the Cycle of Life becomes, with the additional length of the vertical beam, a cross of suffering, sometimes death. Thus the elongated cross shape seems to suggest not only life and death, but the inevitable turmoil, strife, and conflict of our life/death dramas. Interestingly, strife and conflict are seen as the prime qualities of the Air/Swords suit of the Tarot. This "enlightenment/self-awareness" stuff isn't easy; when we become aware of something we are required to take on some measure of responsibility concerning it!

What we are seeing here is the dual nature of Life Itself and of the Sun God (or Goddess if you like); he is god of life and also of death. The Cycle of Life brings both life and death. Death is a part of life in that from death comes life; from the Land of Death/Spirit, we are born into Life/Matter; and dead plant matter (compost) fertilizes the soil for new life/growth. From the darkness comes the light: from a dark sky the sun rises, its beautiful, warm colors gradually replacing the colder colors of night's darkness.

The power of the Sword is the power of defining boundaries, for example, the boundaries between light and darkness; truth and falsehood; knowledge and ignorance; this world and the other worlds. Separating one thing from another is sometimes a necessary act and is essential to creation. We cast the circle with a Sword in Traditional Wicca, defining, for ourselves, boundaries between the worlds, thereby creating a sacred space.

The arrow can also be associated with the Element of Air. Shot into the air from a bow toward a target beyond, it is carried by and through the air by the force of the shooting forth. Thus the arrow is analogous to the carrying of our ideas and thoughts beyond ourselves—by and through the air, and by the power of vibration—toward their destined targets.

So again, the characteristics of East are those of origination: sprouting, beginning, movement. The power of East is the power of the Sun at the beginning of its time of ascendancy, and the power of the Earth at the beginning of its cycle of new life. It is the power of illumination and clarity: dawn, daybreak, the ability to see clearly now that light has come. The time of Spring is a time of springing forth, from the darkness of Winter or of night, to the brightness and mild warmth of the new day and the promise of renewed life.

ELEMENTAL BEING—SYLPH

The magical beings associated with the Element of Air are the *Sylphs*, perhaps from the Latin word "*silphe*" referring to a winged insect. They are envisioned as delicate, beautiful, winged creatures, but it's important to remember that these beings are *energies,* and to remain open to whatever form they may choose to assume. This is especially true in this case. Sylphs, being elementals of Air, are changeable, like the wind, and may assume a different appearance than you are expecting if you have allowed yourself to get locked into a particular idea of their appearance. The Sylphs' natural habitat is the air, thus their work is about maintaining the purity and integrity of the planet's atmosphere. With this in mind, reflecting on the human-caused problems of air pollution and holes in the ozone layer becomes even more sobering. Sylphs do the same for us on an individual level, helping in the maintenance and integrity of our mental bodies.

THE SEASONAL TIDES AND PRECESSION OF THE EQUINOXES

In the Celtic tradition of Wicca, Spring is said to begin at Imbolc, the Feast of Brigit, rather than at the Spring Equinox, and Brigit has long been honored and invoked as the Goddess of Inspiration. So much of the springlike flavor of the Imbolc feast—including the role played by Inspiration—is equally applicable to the Spring Equinox. Celebrate these occasions when it is seasonally appropriate to where you live.

Actually, the way I like to think of and work with these energies is by use of what is referred to in some of the old traditions as the "Seasonal Tides." Our distant ancestors were tuned to the rhythm of Earth and Sky: the length of day and night, the disappearance/reappearance of certain stars (or star groups) and planets, the life cycles of the plants and animals. These illustrated clearly the Seasonal Tides, the path and manner of Nature's cyclic, flowing power. The Tides begin and end at the Greater Sabbats of Imbolc, Beltane, Lughnasadh, and Samhain, with the Solstice and Equinox points marking the peak of power of the seasons (see page 64). Despite the fact that, scientifically speaking, the solstices and equinoxes are said to mark the start and finish of the seasons, I prefer to use them as the seasonal midpoints, marking seasonal beginnings and endings with the Greater Sabbats as indicated by the Tides. For a much more detailed treatment

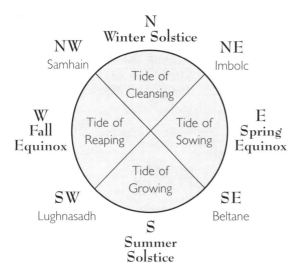

Wheel of the Seasonal Tides

In the diagram:
- N — Winter Solstice
- NW — Samhain
- NE — Imbolc
- W — Fall Equinox
- E — Spring Equinox
- SW — Lughnasadh
- SE — Beltane
- S — Summer Solstice

Inner quadrants: Tide of Cleansing (top), Tide of Reaping (left), Tide of Sowing (right), Tide of Growing (bottom)

of this subject, see Patricia Crowther's excellent book *Lid Off the Cauldron* (see Bibliography).

As previously mentioned, the Celts, as well as other of our ancestors, were known to have counted their "day" as beginning the night before (i.e., sunset, twilight), and it seems likely that this was how they regarded their seasons also. Thus Imbolc, regarded as the beginning of Spring, would represent this "twilight" period of time, just as Samhain "Eve" (All Hallow's Eve/Halloween) is regarded as the *beginning* of the feast of Samhain (which continues till sunset the next day, November 1). The actual feast of Samhain is/was regarded as the *beginning* of the *Season* of Winter.

Another factor that enters into this discussion of which particular Sabbat is most appropriately connected with the beginning and end of which season, is a phenomenon known as the Precession of the Equinoxes. Due to the gravitational pull of the sun and the moon on the earth's equatorial bulge, the earth's spinning motion is subject to a slow wobble. Through the course of time, this wobble changes the appearance of the positions of the stars in the night sky. The earth's North-South axis (the imaginary line that extends North-South

through the body of the planet and infinitely beyond in both directions) appears—over the course of approximately 26,000 years—to perform a slow circle dance through the sky, returning at the end of this time to the point where the dance began. This circle dance, called the Precession of the Equinoxes, is the reason why the North Star changes through the Ages. Polaris (alpha Ursae Minoris) is our current North Star; a few thousand years ago it was beta Ursae Minoris (in the constellation of Ursa Minor, as is Polaris). Five thousand years ago it was Thuban (Alpha Draconis) in the constellation of Draco. In 12,500 years or so, the North Star will be Vega in the constellation Lyra.

It is this circle dance that creates the Zodiacal Ages, as the sun appears to rise within a different constellation (of the twelve well-known, irregularly sized and shaped constellations positioned around earth's ecliptic plane) every 2,160 years. With twelve constellations, each 2,160-year period is like a "month" in the 26,000 year "Great Year." The direction of this motion through our twelve constellations is opposite that of the yearly course of the sun. Thus while the Sun appears to move from Aries into Taurus, then Gemini, and so on (or clockwise), the precessional movement is from Aries to Pisces, then Aquarius (counterclockwise). It is interesting to note that other Zodiacs exist in the Lakota and Mayan traditions, for instance, with their own star-pattern constellations, and their own acknowledgment of the Turning of the Ages.

For further detail on this phenomena, consult a good astronomy book, which will give greater detail and definition of terms than I can in this short description.

The significance of this astronomical data to us, though, is that it has been over 3,000 years since the Spring Equinox Sun truly rose in 0 degrees of the constellation of Aries, though we still count it as such on our astro-calendars. Currently, our Equinox sunrise is in the early degrees of the Water sign of Pisces. Long ago when the significance of the times we now call the "Greater

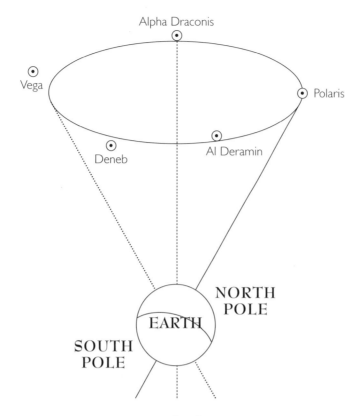

Precessional of Equinoxes

Sabbats" (November 1, February 1, May 1, and August 1) was first recognized, perhaps these dates did indeed correspond to the Solstice and Equinox points at which the seasons of the year are said to officially begin and end. If so, this was a very long time ago; in fact, since we are poised on the brink of the "Age of Aquarius," it would have been nearly 21,000 years ago!

In the soon to dawn "Age of Aquarius" (different sources give different dates for this—most of them within the next 20 to 200 years), the Spring Equinox sun will be rising within Aquarius—the Air sign of the Zodiac whose airy qualities of movement, originality, and inspiration seem to link it to the festival of Imbolc/Spring.

The precession describes the relationship of Earth with the Stars; and the effects of an "Age" are manifested over long periods of time—the 2,160-year length of the Age. Earth's relationship with

the Sun, which defines our Seasons, remains constant. Spring is Spring (and springtime energies are springtime energies!)—no matter what sign within which the Sun is seen to rise.

The fact of the Precession of the Equinoxes brings up interesting questions in the field of astrological interpretation (among them questions about the attributes assigned to the various constellations of the Zodiac), but these are beyond the scope of this book; I shall leave professional astrologers to puzzle out these questions and their answers.

It is interesting to me that although we *know* that our Spring Equinox Sun rises in the early degrees of Pisces rather than 0 Aries, conditions here on Earth at the time of the Spring Equinox certainly *seem* to largely reflect the active, fiery, "charging-ahead" energies of Aries rather than the watery Piscean depths. So it would seem that what is going on here is on more than one level.

TRADITIONAL CHINESE MEDICINE AND THE AIR ELEMENT

In TCM there is no Element of Air as such. Instead we find Air's qualities and correspondences spread between two "elements" unique to the Chinese system: Wood and Metal.

Air feeds Fire, Air being necessary for combustion to occur. So too does wood feed Fire: it provides the needed fuel. In the TCM system of reckoning, Wood comes prior to (and is said to "generate," or be the "Mother of") Fire. The Wood element is associated with the Spring and the color associated with it is the vibrant green we see in Spring. The Liver is the major associated organ. The Liver (whose energy is said to flow upwards in the Spring, just as does the sap of a tree) is rightfully called "*Live*-r"—because we could not *live* without it! It has a tremendous number of functions within the body (and is involved directly or indirectly in just about all physiological processes), but when it does its job correctly, the result is that things are kept *moving* smoothly along; there's that quality of movement/change again.

The Metal element is concerned with the taking in and giving out processes associated with the Air Element. Its associated organs are the lungs, which both take in and give out Air, and the large intestine, whose main function is to receive into itself then eliminate from the body, that which is unnecessary (though it is also the site where we absorb water and minerals). In both lungs and large intestine, the energetic movement is said to be downward. Because the Metal Element has a receiving function, we can associate it with the Air Element; but because Metal's eliminative functions (of air and bodily waste) predominate over its receiving functions, Metal is more associated with Autumn, the time of harvest and endings, than it is with Spring. In TCM Metal is said to control the Wood element. This means that its functions serve as a balancing agent to the upward and outward energy of the Wood element, lest it get out of control.

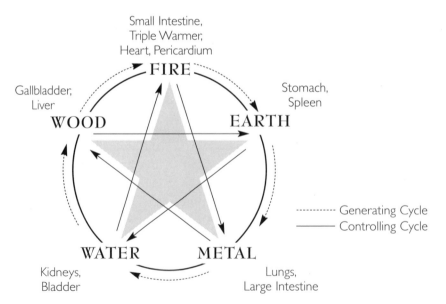

Wheel of the Five Chinese Elements

CHAKRAS
AND THE AIR ELEMENT

As stated in the previous chapter, various systems of thought assign the Air Element to various chakras, the usual ones being the third, *Solar Plexus* chakra (because of its relationship with Mind), the fourth, *Heart* chakra (because of Air's relationship with the power of connecting as well as the physiological relationship between heart and lungs), and the fifth, *Throat* chakra (because of Air's association with sound-speech-hearing and communication).

Both the Solar Plexus chakra (third) and the Heart chakra (fourth) are in the center, vital-organ-containing part of our body. The nearby lungs work in tandem with the heart by supplying oxygen to the blood which flows through the heart, thus keeping it beating. Both heart and lungs are rhythmic and have giving and receiving functions. The Solar Plexus area contains a nexus of nerves as well as being the major nadi (channel for subtle energies in the body) center of the body. Thus energy flows out from this place also. With our arms and hands, traditionally and astrologically associated with the Air Element, we reach out to others: we give, receive, self-express in the form of writing and hand/arm movement.

All of these are Air functions, yet in the same way that there is a relationship between sword and wand—Air and Fire of the magical tools—there is a relationship here: Fire cannot burn without Air. This central, vital-organ-containing part of the body is the place where the Air of inspiration fuels the Fires of life, and perhaps should be considered as a single area combining the qualities of both. I will leave it to the chakra experts to sort out, if possible, whether the Element of Air is rightfully assigned to the third or the fourth Chakra.

AIR CORRESPONDENCES

Colors associated with the Element of Air are white, pale yellow, and sometimes sky blue. Air is clear (at least outside of major cities), so the colors associated with it aren't really "Air" colors in the same way as the colors of the other Elements describe that element. Rather, the colors assigned to Air are associated with the direction of East (pale yellow of the youthful Sun; white for the purity of beginnings) and of the sky, which is of an apparent blue, and Air-filled.

Planets associated with the Air Element are Mercury (ruler of the air sign of Gemini, who wore winged sandals and was said to be the messenger of the gods), and Uranus (astrologically considered to be a higher octave of Mercury's energy, rules electricity and co-rules the air sign of Aquarius). Interestingly, the figure who in Greek myth was known as Uranus (Ouranos) and in Roman myth as Coelus is known to be the most ancient of all the gods; his name means something akin to "overhanging heavens" (i.e., the sky above).

Herbs associated with Air are those ruled by Mercury; i.e., dill, elecampane, fenugreek, flax, horehound, lavender, marjoram, mushroom, senna, trefoil, valerian. Think also of plants whose seeds are distributed primarily by wind, plants who have slender graceful leaves and stems that sway easily in the wind, and plants whose medicinal action relieves, or in some way deals with excess or deficient wind/air.

Stones. If it is indeed possible for the most subtle element (Air) to be represented by an object of the most solid element (Earth), then some stones associated with Air Element would be those that chakra experts and crystal healers associate with the third and fourth chakras: green jade (brings clarity and wisdom; said to be helpful for teachers and speakers), turquoise (whose color is reminiscent of the sky; brings balance), aventurine (said to bring unlimited possibilities by opening us to vast horizons), and citrine (which brings balance of mind by dispelling negativity and aiding relaxation). I remind you to tune into the stones themselves in deciding which ones are representative, for you, of the Air Element.

AIR PRACTICES

AIR ALTARS

Altars devoted to Air, in and of itself, are very hard to imagine. Since Air is colorless, invisible, and only observable when in motion, it's a bit hard to build an altar around. Using the categories we used in *Chapter Two* for Earth Altars, however, also helps us here.

Air Element (pure and simple)

When building an Air altar I use things with Air-related symbolism. Birds, for instance, fly (movement) through the air, so feathers always find their way onto my altar to represent the Element of Air. The drifting smoke of incense is considered to be representative of Air, so I always have incense of some kind on my Air altar. My altar cloth is usually white or pale yellow, and I fill the altar with not only the above-mentioned feathers and incense, but also the stones and plants of the Air element and astrological symbolism representing Air (Mercury and Uranus). In addition, sometimes the Tarot cards of the King or Queen of Swords find their way there, swords being representative of Air in the Tarot.

Air Season/Spring

This would be similar to the altar above, but keyed to the season of Spring. This opens up possibilities of beautiful spring flowers of various colors; branches just beginning to leaf out; a small sun disk; feathers; images of butterflies, other winged beings, and sylphs; and trees blowing in spring breezes.

Here is a meditation to help you connect with the Element of Air. It helps if you can read it into a tape recorder to play for yourself later on, thus allowing you to close your eyes and sink deeply into an altered state while you experience it.

Ideally, this meditation should be done outside on a windy day, with no props but your imagination. If that is not possible, opt for the following.

AIR ELEMENT MEDITATION

PREPARATION

For this meditation you will need to have incense burning, so get this set up and ready to go. If you wish you may substitute sage, but you will have to relight it each time during the meditation you wish to interact with it, since it tends to go out after a few minutes. Keep your container of incense handy so that you can replenish your incense burner's supply when necessary.

If you desire to do this meditation in a formal, ritual space, the area should be decorated in Air colors and motifs. Cloths of white, pale yellows, and blue are suitable for the altar and for wall hangings. Representations of air creatures—birds, butterflies, clouds, and sylphs—should be present in statue, pendant, or picture form, as well as the above-mentioned herbs and stones. Tarot Cards from the Suit of Swords can also be used. Decorate the room with feathers, wind chimes, and anything else you can think of that seems "airy" to you. Perhaps you may want to open a door or window if there is a breeze blowing outside. When all is ready, the ceremony may be begun by casting a circle, if desired.

INDUCTION

Get yourself comfortable. Close your eyes, take a deep breath, and relax. Continue to breathe slowly and deeply and feel yourself getting more and more relaxed and comfortable. With each breath you take in, you feel yourself becoming more relaxed. With each breath you breathe out, you feel yourself letting go of the cares and concerns of the day, breathing out what is no longer needed. Become aware of your body, feel yourself sitting upon your chair or floor. As you breathe slowly and deeply, become aware of the feeling of your own energy.

Continue to breathe slowly as you allow your mind to calm itself and to grow clear and still. As you read or hear the words that follow, allow them to create images within your mind. Allow the images to become alive, full of light, color, sound, and movement, all as indicated by the words of this guided meditation. Enter the pictures now formed and become part of the unfolding experience.

AIR MEDITATION

You are standing outside on the top of a very high mountain. There are flowering plants growing at your feet, grasses, shrubs, and some tall trees near where you stand. Several yards away some deer are munching on the shrubs, and overhead birds circle lazily in the sky. The view is wonderful; you can see for many miles around you. The day is clear and bright, and the sky is scattered with cream puffs of clouds.

As you look around and see what there is to see, you become aware that a breeze has sprung up. It is a gentle, refreshing breeze and it brings a cool pleasing feeling as it blows upon you, causing your hair to blow back from your face. This breeze carries sounds on it; you hear the cries of birds flying overhead, a distant sound of someone playing a flute, and of course, the quiet whooshing sound of the breeze itself. This breeze also carries aromas. In particular you find that the scent of some of the plants and trees around you have suddenly grown a bit stronger. You close your inner eyes, so that you

may feel, smell, and hear this breeze for a few moments. (PAUSE)

When you open your inner eyes, it is to find that the sky has changed. Many more clouds are in the sky now, and you spend some time examining their shapes. You become aware that the wind is picking up; what was a gentle, pleasant breeze has become a goodly breeze. It begins to toss around leaves that have fallen to the ground and swirl them around in little circles. Soon little clouds of dust are being whipped up into similar swirling circles and the wind continues to rise.

The shapes of the clouds change rapidly now as they move quickly through the sky, in concert with the wind. Your hair is blowing into a tangled mess and you find it hard to keep your eyes open due to the swirling dust. The wind seems to whip toward you, coming from one direction, then another, then yet another. It seems to want to toss you about.

Suddenly the wind gathers itself in one of the directions and rises up tremendously, shrieking and howling, seeming to penetrate and permeate you, blowing so hard it is almost impossible to stand up straight, so you don't even attempt to. You turn to face the wind and allow it to support your body as you lean into it. Take a few moments and experience what it feels like to have the wind support you in this way. (PAUSE)

As you experience this, you are suddenly aware that the wind seems to be alive—its voice, many voices all at once. As you feel it whip around you, through you, you feel the presence of many beings, and know you are experiencing the presence of the Air Elementals known as Sylphs.

After a few moments, the wind begins to die down again, its howling subsiding into whistles and whispers and a few sudden gusts. You open your eyes and find that as you watch the dust and leaf swirls that are still dancing around your feet, they seem to you to be Beings: insubstantially bodied Beings, but Beings nonetheless. You can feel their "beingness" even as your eyes struggle to catch and hold their ceaselessly moving, changing forms.

As your awareness of these Beings increases, you realize they are also aware of you; and now the gusts of wind begin to swirl around and around your body, from toe to head, moving skyward. As this happens you are simultaneously aware of a sense of exhilaration and excitement that seems to rise as the winds, rising again, spiral around you moving skyward. You become aware of your own vibrational frequency now, because you can feel it rising along with the wind. Faster and faster the Sylphs dance around you, the winds whip around you, till you find yourself twirling and whirling right along with them and dancing and laughing in delight.

Suddenly the wind gathers itself again and rises up higher, stronger, moaning and shrieking. The Sylphs continue to swirl around you but the dance is different now. Somehow you do not feel such delight and glee. The wind begins to form itself into a swirling, spiraling vortex; its power increases. Suddenly this spiraling vortex lifts you into the air, swirls you rapidly several times and tosses you out to land several feet away upon the ground. Thankfully, the grass and plants receive you, rather than the rocky ground, so you are not hurt. As you pick yourself up off of the ground, a single feather, white with swirls of black upon it, drifts to the ground and lands at your feet. You know it is a gift from the Beings with whom you have just interacted; just to look at it reminds you of their extremely changeable, unpredictable nature. You pick up the feather, and brush it lightly across your hand. Holding the feather, sit for a few

moments, with the realization of Air's true nature. (PAUSE)

As this realization sinks into you, you feel something inside of you resonate in response. Reach into yourself now, feeling into your bodies physical and subtle, into the spaces where things whirl and swirl, move and connect, inhale, exhale; feeling into your mind, thoughts, and feelings. Find the place (or places) inside you that is Air/wind. With the help of the Sylph's gift in your hand, feel this Air-ness that is inside of you; feel its insubstantiality, changeability, lack of solid stable form, its weightlessness, its speed of movement; its power of piercing and penetration. Touch this part of yourself. Go inside of it, merge with it, let there be no separation. Spend some time doing this. (PAUSE) Give thanks for the part within you that is Air.

Without altering your state of consciousness, open your outer eyes now for a few moments, that you may place more incense into your incense burner, or light your piece of sage. As it burns, allow yourself to experience both the aroma of the incense and to watch the patterns the smoke makes as it rises. Watch these patterns and allow your mind to drift with them for a while.

Realize that the Air Beings—the Sylphs, the Beings of breath, air, of mind, of wind, of change—live also within you, throughout your bodies physical and subtle, but very much so in the processes of your mind. They are the forces that keeps things moving, changing, circulating. Send your love and gratitude to the Sylphs for the many jobs they do and for the love they have for you.

As you continue to watch the smoke patterns and smell the scent of incense, you become aware that, within you, your mind and memory have been awakened. As the smoke drifts, the shapes it forms begin to remind you of many things; some things recognizable, but some long since forgotten.

Allow yourself to simply experience this flow of swirling patterns, thoughts, and memories. Observe how this feels. Realize how similar it is to the pattern of your own thoughts as they move and swirl through your mind. As you do this, see how, though the drifting, swirling patterns seem aimless, they move in such a fashion as to connect not only with each other, but with everything else that is there as they move, swirl, and drift upward and outward, curling themselves around solid substances, penetrating the more permeable of substances. Think of how permeable substances such as cloth are able to take on scents carried by air, such as that of incense.

As you think of these things, lean forward toward the smoke of the incense and look at it for another moment. In this moment, allow this smoke to represent all the air that is outside of you. Now, consciously, smudge yourself with it, breathing it in as much as is comfortable to you, receiving it into yourself. Be aware of its scent, of the way it makes your nose and throat feel, its temperature, any sensations it may bring to you. Be aware of it as Air, as Earth's atmosphere, a rare and wondrous combination of gases appropriate to our survival. As you are thinking these things, feel yourself merging with the air you have just inhaled—and continue to inhale and exhale. Continue breathing in both the air and these realizations.

Close your eyes once again. Be aware also that as you breathe in, you are inhaling into your body the air Beings who live within the Air, as you unite the outer smoke/incense/air with your inner mind/movement air.

Feel your union with Air. *You are Air.* Merge yourself with this realization so that it is inside of you. Feel it moving through you at great speed as it penetrates both your subtle bodies and your physical organs and cells. Follow its movement with your awareness, be one with it rather than separate. Realize that because Air moves, penetrates, and permeates, it unites inside and outside; the boundaries between them are as insubstantial as Air itself. *You are Air.* Feel yourself swirl, whirl, drift, permeate, penetrate. And as you feel yourself moving, know yourself as movement, and in that knowing, realize you are carried to the heart of the Great Mystery.

Remain centered in this knowing as you allow yourself to become more aware of your surroundings. Allow your breathing to return to normal, and when you are ready you may open your eyes.

AIR EXERCISES

1. Go outside, properly clad, on a particularly windy day. Stand out in the wind, feeling its power, watching it move things as it blows. Feel the exhilaration that it produces in you as it whips your hair and clothing around. Note the temperature of the wind, and try to ascertain the direction from which it is coming, and the "shape" (if any) in which it seems to be blowing. If you can find a wind that blows leaves around in a circle or spiral shape, so much the better. Stay and watch this phenomena for awhile—maybe you will see the Sylphs. Take this opportunity to pray to the Wind Spirits and thank them for the power of movement and change.

2. Use the fact that the Air has the power of movement to experiment with your sense of smell. Light some incense and watch how it drifts into the air, and how the Air carries its smoke and the fragrance to you and beyond.

3. Light some incense as part of a prayer to God or Goddess, and send your prayer upward and outward with the smoke of the incense.

4. Find a good safe place to stand, inside or outside, and begin spinning yourself around (take proper precautions against bumping into things or falling down, please!). Pretend you are a two-year-old and really get into it! When you feel you've done it long enough (and this may only be eight to ten spins), stop, sit down, and allow yourself to experience the giddy whirling feeling that continues for a while afterward. To spin is to create movement; to spin in circles is to simulate the circular/spiraling movement inherent in the creation of life.

5. Develop an awareness of, and thankfulness toward, Air. When you hang your clothes out to dry, or turn on the clothes drier, when you hook up your electric fan during the Summer, or turn on the fan over the kitchen stove, be mindful of and thankful to the Powers of Air. Take a slow deep breath, and feel the air fill your lungs. Take this breath with the awareness that it is the Breath of Life. Exhale with the awareness that you are exhaling that which is not needed. Give thanks to the Beings of Air for the Breath of Life. Try to be aware of the gifts of the Air Element and the Breath of Life every now and then throughout the day. Keep wind chimes near your back door so that even a gentle breeze has a voice for you to hear. When you are thus reminded of Air, give thanks to the Powers of Air.

6. Go outside some breezy day, and watch the wind as it blows through the branches of the trees. Watch the different qualities of movement the branches make in response to the wind. Watch the wind as it whirls dry leaves around and around in circles. Look up into the sky and spend some time watching the movement of the clouds.

7. Go fly a kite! Really! Though it's hard work to get a kite off of the ground, once you get it airborne, you'll be able to experience, through the kite's movement and the feel of the string, the differences in each of the levels of air movement and currents.

8. For the truly adventurous types, things like hot air balloon rides, hang glider flight, sailboats (all with proper instruction, of course, instruction being a crucial Air Element correspondence), and other dramatic ways of interacting with Air can be very physical ways of learning about the Air Element.

9. When you feel your life is really in need of some changes, make an altar to the Four Winds and do a ceremony to invoke the winds of positive change into your life, fine-tuning it to the particular qualities of the particular Direction and Element most needed. Make offerings to the Winds, and be respectful. Be as specific as you can be in your request—you never know what the wind might bring!

10. Compose an invocation to the Powers of the Air Element. Work with what you have learned and discovered about the nature of this element and work at reducing it into a few relevant and personally meaningful words. Write it in poetic form if you like, or

even in the form of a song or chant. Make it short and simple enough to be easily committed to memory, and let it reflect your personal feelings of appreciation and love for the Element.

11. Think! Use your mind! Study something, and really think about what you're learning. Observe your mind at work, as it takes in the new information, reacts to it, organizes it, relates it to other information previously processed, and in general, works with and seeks to understand the new information. It's an interesting process to behold; even more interesting when feelings come up about what's being learned.

12. Spend some time sitting and just breathing, letting your thoughts flow where they will.

Practice stepping outside of them and just watching them as they move, jumping from one thing to another, by way of the associations and correspondences previously established. I must admit, this takes practice; noting the pathways your thoughts have traveled is often easier *after* the fact.

13. Ask yourself the following questions, and really think about them:

- What things in my life are being born or reborn, or getting new life?
- What elements in my life *feel* like they need rebirth? How does this feel?
- What things in my life provide inspiration to me?

SEASONAL MEDITATION: SENSING SPRING

This is an activity to help you connect with the powers that are flowing through nature at this time of the year: Springtime. According to our calendar, Springtime stretches (in the Northern Hemisphere) from March 21, the Spring Equinox, until June 21, the Summer Solstice. This is the official astronomical timing of the Spring season, beginning on the day of equal light and dark, even though the Wiccan Wheel of the Year notes Imbolc (February 1) as the beginning of Spring. How Spring manifests depends where you live. In my area, early to mid-February brings indication that Spring is on its way. So please use this activity whenever it feels like the right time to do so.

Pick a Spring day that is especially beautiful and mild, with blue sky and brilliant sunshine. Find a place in your backyard or in a nearby park where you can be alone and undisturbed for a while. This location should feel like a good place to you; it should call to you to come and be there. The place should be full of the new, green, growing things of Spring: grass, the early blooming flowers of your area, a tree with budding or new leaves on it. Perhaps you can even find an area that includes some of the baby animals of Spring: baby birds, tadpoles, lambs, or chicks.

When you have found your place stand there for a few moments and settle yourself into it. Close your eyes and take a deep breath, then let it out slowly. Keep breathing slowly as you feel yourself becoming calm, and feel your energy coming into alignment with the energy of your location. Feel your aura (the energy field around your body) growing and expanding outward to touch all that is around you. Use your imagination to do this. Simply imagine a glowing field of light around your body, that grows larger or smaller as you wish it to. Picture this in your mind.

In your mind, draw around yourself a golden circle of protective light and thank God and Goddess for the privilege of being part of such a beautiful planet. Ask the Devas and Nature Spirits to come and be with you and help you appreciate the beauty and wonder of the Earth.

Now, open your eyes and look around at everything. Look at the blue sky and clouds above you, the green Earth beneath you, the growing things around you—grasses, weeds, flowers, and leaves. Look at it all slowly and carefully, noticing the beautiful, living colors; noticing the way the light touches everything, the patterns of light and shadow. Look at each thing separately and then at how it looks all together. Just look at it all and drink it into yourself, as if this colorful beauty was a nourishing drink for your soul, as indeed it is. Use your breath and breathe it all into you. Take time doing this, and when you are finished give thanks for what you have seen, and give thanks for the gift of sight.

Focus now on your sense of smell. Begin sniffing, and noticing which smells and aromas are present. Can you smell the damp, fresh aroma of the Earth? Or perhaps the Earth is not damp and it is a drier, earthy smell you are noticing? If you are near the ocean can you smell the saltiness in the air? If you are near a stream or pond what scents do you detect from these places? Can you smell the grasses and flowers nearby, or the trees? Now smell these fragrances all together and breathe them into you, allowing them to flow through your whole body with the movement of your breath. Feel nourished by them. When you are finished, give thanks for what you have smelled, and give thanks for the gift of smell.

Look around for a plant that you know is safe to eat, such as sourgrass, plantain, borage flowers, or violets. If you can find nothing you absolutely know to be safe, skip this part of the meditation and go on to the next part. If you find something safe to nibble, ask the plant's permission to pick just one flower or leaf. Just one. If you get a feeling inside you that the plant is giving you permission to nibble it, say thank you to the plant, send it love, then pick the flower or leaf. Close your eyes now and slowly nibble on the piece of plant, feeling your mouth come alive with the taste sensations. Is it sweet, salty, sour, bitter, spicy? Or does it have a mixture of these tastes? Does it taste good to you? Or not so good? Or maybe just new and unusual? As you continue to chew, feel the taste as it swirls through your mouth. Enjoy the experience, even if the taste is one that you are not used to! You are tasting the life force as it flows through this particular plant being, expressing itself in this particular way. When you have finished tasting, then chew and swallow this piece of plant, taking it into you as the holy thing that it is. Give thanks to the plant for sharing itself with you. Give thanks for what you have tasted, and give thanks for the gift of taste.

Now close your eyes again and listen to the sounds of Spring around you. Listen carefully to each and every sound. Are there dogs barking? Are there birds singing, crickets chirping, people talking? Can you hear the wind in the trees, the sound of water flowing, or the soft rustle of plants blowing in a breeze? If you listen carefully, can you hear the sap running in the trees, or perhaps hear the sound of the plants growing? Listen, listen to all the sounds around you. Then separate them out and listen to each sound separately; then listen to them all together again, as if they were an orchestra playing a symphony for you. Drink this into you, these sounds of Spring; breathe them in with your breath. Take your time doing this. When you are finished, give thanks for what you have heard, and give thanks for the gift of hearing.

Lie down now upon the ground and begin to feel what is under and around you. First of all, feel yourself as you lie upon the ground. What does your body feel like now? Are you comfortable or not? Cold, hot, or just right? Happy, excited, or calm? Now feel the ground on which you are lying. Is it hard or soft beneath you? Does it feel smooth, grassy, sandy, bumpy, rocky? Is it dry or damp? What does the upper surface of your body, the side of you that is not in contact with the ground, feel like now? Is there a breeze blowing? Can you feel the warmth of the sun as it shines on you? Or are you in the shade, and feeling a comfortable, or perhaps uncomfortable, sense of coolness? Have ants or other little critters discovered you lying there and decided to crawl on you? Let your aura expand very much during this activity. Reach out with your aura, using your imagination to do so, because reaching out with your aura will allow you to feel more. Reach out beneath you now with your aura, so that part of your aura is allowed to sink down into the earth and feel it. What does the earth slightly below the surface feel like to you? Does it feel solid, heavy, and slow, or light, quick, and flowing? All of these, some of these, or something totally different? Feel the earth energies as they surge upward from deep inside the earth to show themselves as the vibrant growth and color of Spring. Reach your hands out now and connect with what is around you on the ground. Pick up a rock or twig, run your palms over a patch of grass, finger the stems of a plant, or pull gently on a blade of grass. Let your fingers trace the roughness of a tree trunk or root. Allow yourself to feel this, with both your physical sense of touch and with your energy sensing abilities. Drink these sensations into you, breathe them in with your breath. When you are finished, give thanks for what you have felt and sensed, and give thanks for the gift of feeling.

Can you feel how you are part of everything you have seen, tasted, smelled, heard, touched, and felt? (PAUSE) You are part of it all, yet you are your own unique self, too.

Open your eyes as you lie upon the ground. Be aware of what all your senses are bringing to you. Look up at the sky, then all around. Taste the lingering taste of the plant in your mouth, sniff the fragrances and aromas around you, listen to the sounds surrounding you, feel the Earth beneath you and the energies of the plants and Nature Spirits all around you.

Feel your own energy running inside of you and let it fountain forth from the top of your head, from your hands and feet (don't forget to use your imagination if you need to when doing this). Feed it to the world around you. Share yourself with all that has shared itself with you. Once again, give thanks to the trees, the plants, the animals, the wind, the water, and the sky. Give thanks also to the Nature Spirits and the God and Goddess. Tuck this experience safely inside you, to remember forever, and bid the plants and trees farewell, with love and gratitude in your heart.

When you feel ready, get up and go home.

CHAPTER FOUR

Fire

The Element of Fire is one with which we are all familiar as a source of heat and light in our lives. Whether it be the fires by which we cook and heat our homes, or the light by which we read our book, the powers of fire, light, and heat are ones we could not live without. Yet out of control, the power of fire is a source of great destruction. Fire's nature is active: flames flicker and move fast; coals stay hot and dangerous longer than firefighters wish they would. The same fire that warms us and by which we cook can, when out of control, destroy us. With constant light and no darkness, the principle of expansion would go wild. We would become overstimulated, and find it difficult to rest and relax.

WESTERN MYSTERY TRADITION AND THE FIRE ELEMENT

DIRECTION—SOUTH

As you may know, in the Western Mystery Tradition of which Wicca is a part, Fire is assigned to the Southern Quarter of the Circle.

South is the place of Summer, of creativity and growth; of strength and innocence, youthfulness, and trust. It is the place of spirit, of energy; of life and life's blood. It is the place where life's powerful intention to "*be*" is strongly in evidence all around us in nature. Because of all these associations, it is also the place of *will* (see Magician's Wheel, page 22).

The South is known as the place of the Mystery of the Volcano, the mystery of new life created from Earth's inner, stellar fires. It is the mystery of how Earth's Heart/ Hearthfires, rise up to the surface, bringing rich and fertilizing influences in the form of magma. Although volcanoes may initially destroy or alter the existing order of things, over the course of time they always result in new life and growth. The Mystery of the Volcano is about the rising and emergence of the inner Star Fires of Creation, whether within the Earth or within our own beings. On the level of our physical bodies, our sexual fires are representative of this. Within our subtle bodies, it is the coiled, sleeping serpent-dragon, the Goddess power known as Kundalini, which awakens and rises up, uncoiling through the chakras, bringing awakening and enlightenment as she passes. The Mystery of the Volcano, whose physical counterpart can sleep for many years then suddenly erupt into life, encompasses the mysteries of consciousness awakening, rising up, illumination, and the Powers of Creation, Life, and Growth.

South is the place of the brightest and strongest light, the Sun in full strength. Therefore South is associated with the season of Summer and the time of noon: midday, when the sun is directly overhead. Both Summer and midday are times of wakefulness and work—hard work requiring strength of several sorts—in order to have things ready for the harvest by the time Autumn rolls around. The daylight hours are the longest during Summer, allowing more time for this wakefulness and work. If you take the old Celtic Calendar reckoning that says that Summer begins on Beltane, then the Summer Solstice falls in the middle of Summer. The time of longest light spreads on either side of this day, which is probably why one of the old names for the Summer Solstice was midsummer, and the correspondence between midday and midsummer becomes more understandable.

The South is the place of the Soul. The Soul is our *personal* indwelling vehicle of *spirit*. The Soul is as much a part of the totality of our beingness as are body, mind, and emotions. Our soul is the "function-modality" of our spirits-in-physicality. Souls are spirits with a destiny to be worked out within a physical body. "Soul" has qualities of feeling, depth, and perception to it; all of these are, of course, qualities of consciousness. It is thought that after death the soul is subject to disintegration just as is the body, though our individualized spark of spirit lives on, richer and wiser from the experiences gained.

There is a clear, brilliant quality about this direction of South—just as the brilliance of the dazzling, midday Sun reduces shadows to minimum. As the sunlight grows strongest at midday, the fiery powers of fertility, creation, and growth are strongest and most available to us from the South. Because of all this, the South is also the place of the *will* as in the magical maxim "to know, to will, to dare, to keep silent." By the way, the *will* is not simply our use of willpower to "muscle" our way through situations and/or our desires into being. Will is, at its best, spirit working with (our) soul to express its truth through the vehicle of our lives and destinies. Will is our intention, our inner striving to grow toward our highest destiny.

MAGICAL TOOL—WAND

The magical tool for the South is the wand. At this point, however, I must refer back to the previously mentioned difference of opinion as to whether the wand or the sword is representative of the South/Fire (or the East/Air). A case can be made for either tool, in my opinion. However, I feel more comfortable using the wand as the magical tool for the South, as the wielding of it seems more associated with the quality of will associated with the direction of South than does sword-wielding. On Tarot cards the wands pictured on the Suit of Wands (also referred to as "rods") are made of wood, and are depicted leafing out, thus showing the characteristics of growth and creativity.

In popular mythology the wand is associated with various wizardly types and is always associated with will: It is used by pointing it at someone or something to engender change (Cinderella's fairy godmother waves it over her and a new dress, hairdo, and carriage are produced). In Celtic mythology not much is heard about wands, but a lot is heard about the Spear as the tool of the South, in particular the Spear of Lugh, Celtic god associated with the fiery power of the Sun. In this way of thinking, the quality of strength is brought into consideration of South's qualities, and along with strength, victory. Often spears are pictured as wooden-handled tools (like wands) with a stone or metal pointed tip attached. If you picture a wand as a tool through which you direct your will, then a spear is the same or even more so, but with the added qualities of sharpness and precision lent by the sharp tip.

The leafing-out wand shows the power of growth and creativity; the sharp tipped, long-handled spear suggests power, skill, coordination, and strength. One would seem to suggest life, the other death or, at least, conflict. Perhaps what we are seeing here is the dual nature of the Sun god, since he is god of life and also of death. But from death sometimes comes life. The careful wielding of a spear suggests also a lance (as well as the surgeon's knife), used by a healer to cut open an infected wound so that it may drain, and allowing in the heat and drying power of the sun and air, thus heal. So the powers of cleansing and healing are here in the South also.

The powers of the South are those of life: growth, creativity, strength, cleansing, healing, warmth, and fertility, the power of the Sun at its greatest, hottest, brightest strength (see Table of Elemental Correspondences, page 18). The time of Summer is a time of exertion, when both Nature and humans play and work overtime.

ELEMENTAL BEING—SALAMANDER

The magical beings associated with the Element of Fire are the Salamanders. According to Doreen Valiente's *An ABC of Witchcraft Past and Present*, the origin of this word is uncertain, but it possibly derives from the Greek *salambe* meaning fireplace. Salamanders are envisioned as small, red-gold, lizard-like, even dragon-like or snake-like creatures who reside in the flames and among the glowing embers of the fire, but it is important to remember that these beings are energies, and to remain open to whatever form they may choose to assume. We are all familiar with the amphibians known as salamanders: soft, moist creatures seemingly more related to water and earth than to fire. These salamanders are *not* the ones associated with the Element of Fire. It is likely that these creatures gained their name through their superficial resemblance to lizards.

Salamanders reside in the fires of the Earth, and in our fires, and are concerned with all heat functions, from volcanoes and sexuality, to creativity and healing. They are concerned with maintaining the purity and integrity of both the Earth's fire, and our inner fires of spirit/soul.

BRIGIT BEGOIBNE

I'd like to take a brief but relevant detour now, to show you the immense, far-reaching significance of the Element of Fire in the minds and lives of our ancestors. I will give you an example from Ireland, but bear in mind that similar examples can be uncovered in other lands, too.

In Ireland it was believed that Brigit, solar-lunar goddess/saint of inspiration, healing, creativity, and the Hearthfires, had a sister referred to as Brigit Begoibne, or sometimes just Begoibne. She was "the woman of the smithy and the pot maker." Goibniu is the old Irish smith-god, the God of the Fires of the Underworld, and of course smith and pot maker are both intimately related with Fire (using Fire's powers of transformation in their almost magical crafts). Thus Brigit Begoibne was an Underworld Goddess, She of the Infernal Fires at the Heart of the Earth. This Brigit was said to live below the family hearth, and frequently a pot was buried in front of the family hearth, in Her honor. This pot-oven vessel, or cauldron, linked her with the pot maker and the smithy. It represented the abyss, the lower world domain of Brigit, as well as graphically representing the feminine creative powers of the womb. The underworld, represented in this case by the place below the hearth, was also thought to be the domain of the ancestors. The ancestors watch over the family, and in the pagan world view, can quite possibly be reborn into it. The Fire at the Heart of the Earth is the domain of Brigit Begoibne, Queen of the Land of the Dead and the ancestors who lived there; the Hearthfire itself was watched over by Brigit, the golden, "delightful flame," who was also the Goddess of the fiery orb of the Sun and the luminous, cool, cyclical, changing fire of the moon. It is not surprising to find she was also the "Matron" goddess/saint of childbirth.

TRADITIONAL CHINESE MEDICINE AND THE FIRE ELEMENT

In TCM mention is made of the "fires of digestion," which must burn properly—not too high, not too low, for proper digestion and subsequent nourishment and cell growth to take place. Fire is also associated with love and sexuality, the fires of passion. Creativity on a very physical, sexual level becomes, obviously, the future generation. Everything is energy of one form or another; but fire is pure energy of a formless sort. Touch it and you will feel the sensation of heat and get burned, but your hand will not come in contact with a solid or semi-solid *something*, as when touching earth or water. Fire is energy—creative, destructive energy—and therefore earthly fire has its correlates in the fire of the sun and stars, and ultimately in the original fires of the Universe, the subtle level of which I like to call the Cosmic Hearthfire. There is fire at the heart of the earth: the fiery, molten, outer part of earth's core.

Science tells us that our bodies are, as we will see in Chapter 5, mostly composed of water, but it is Fire that energizes us, powers us, runs us, motivates us, and moves us. Our bodies must maintain a certain temperature to function correctly, and health demands that our body temperature stay within a fairly narrow range, or life is endangered. We must be warm enough, but not too warm. We must be able to cool down, but not too much. Our bodily thermostats control this; how we dress and what we eat make significant contributions to it. If we are in ill health, this fact is reflected in the inner thermostat. If we get an infection, this is indicated by the fact that our bodily temperature rises. Of course, inherent here in everything I've said, is a relationship between fire and water, hot and cold, as the basic elements of life, ever seeking to both express themselves, yet be in balance.

As mentioned previously, in TCM the digestive system is often closely linked with the Element of Fire, though it is not thought to be governed by that Element. The organ meridian systems connected with the Fire Element are the Small Intestine Meridian and the Heart Meridian.

Heartfire, Hearthfire; think about it. We gather around our hearthfires for the warmth they provide, as well as the nourishing food cooked there. We sit with our families and share with them the experience of partaking of nourishment, and are nourished by one another's love and fellowship as well. Our Hearts are like our inner hearths, especially when considered from a point of view of providing warmth and nourishment in our lives. In some cultures the heart, rather than the brain, is seen as the seat of consciousness, a mode of being that invites a loving appreciation of all the interwoven relationships that make up the fabric of life, as well as reminding us of the necessity of head and heart working together.

The function of the Small Intestine is to separate the usable elements of food from the unusable, and to absorb nutrients into the bloodstream where they are carried around the body to nourish it. The heart pumps the blood constantly throughout the entire body, carrying this nutrient rich blood wherever it needs to go. Between these two organs and their functions, we are nourished and kept warm. So once again, we see in the Element of Fire, movement and warmth and the sustaining of life.

CHAKRAS AND THE FIRE ELEMENT

Because of the fire within us, we have the power to nourish ourselves, fertilize ourselves (on metaphoric and metaphysic levels), heal ourselves, purify ourselves, and transform ourselves.

Fire is usually connected with the first, second, third, or fourth chakra. Wherever the power of Mars or the Sun is found, there is the power of Fire. Some systems place Mars at the first chakra, some at the second. Both of these placements relate to the fires of creation and sexuality (though there is a "watery" aspect to creation/sexuality also), and the differences in placement may be due to male/female differences. Some systems place the Sun at the third chakra: the solar plexus/will center. Some place it at the fourth: the heart center. A good case can be made for all of these, as I'm sure you can see. As stated in the previous chapter, the center of the body, the third and fourth chakra areas, can be considered as a place of both Fire *and* Air, since fire needs air in order to burn.

FIRE CORRESPONDENCES

Colors associated with the Element of Fire are fire colors: the reds, oranges, yellows, and golds of the hearthflame, candleflame, bonfire, and Sun. Picture these fires, picture Sunrise and Sunset, picture the blood of life, and you get the idea.

Planets associated with the Fire Element are Mars (god of war—a fiery pursuit, and also ruler of the Fire sign of Aries) and the Sun (for obvious reasons; also as ruler of the Fire sign of Leo).

Herbs associated with the Fire Element are those associated with the fiery planets of Mars and the Sun. Examples are basil, garlic, broom, hawthorn, mustard, onion, parsley, pepper, pine, radish, sarsaparilla, sunflower, tarragon, tobacco, woodruff, (Mars); angelica, ash tree, bay, burnet, chamomile, eyebright, heliotrope, lovage, marigold, mistletoe, rosemary, rue, saffron, St. John's wort, (Sun). When picking an herb to represent the Fire Element, I always tend toward an herb with either a spicy, fiery taste (mustard, onion, garlic, etc.) or one whose appearance and coloration suggest the Sun (chamomile, marigold). Also, herbs whose medicinal action is specific to the heart and small intestine meridians (such as hawthorn) or which can be used for conditions related to the power of Fire (burn-treatment herbs such as St. John's wort which can both prevent and treat sunburn) can be considered Fire Element herbs.

The **stone** I primarily associate with Fire is lava rock (from volcanic eruptions); other sources list bloodstone and rubies too. Once again, stones whose coloration suggests Fire may be used to represent Fire. Use your intuition here. Also, rocks classified as igneous are associated with Fire, since igneous rocks are formed by the solidification of magma, whose molten state implies the presence of the powers of heat.

Stones associated with Fire-ascribed chakras (first, second, third, or fourth), or that contain minerals associated with planets linked to the Fire Element (see table below), are generally used to represent the Fire Element. For example, iron is associated with Mars (and the color red), and gold is associated with the Sun. The iron/Mars connection brings strength and power, both good fiery qualities. Iron is found within the red corpuscles of our blood, as carrier of oxygen molecules. If we do not have sufficient iron, we become pale and weak— anemic. The gold/Sun connection is, perhaps, easier to see. Our literature is replete with references to the golden sun, whose rays stream outward like warm and loving arms to enfold the earth. Gold is soft, fairly malleable, more so than other metals. Gold is traditionally associated with the blood (being found in the blood in tiny amounts) and the heart. In Ayurvedic medicine, gold is considered to be "hot" energetically, and is used medicinally as a heart stimulant. In Anthroposophical medicine it is used for improving circulation and increasing warmth. Metaphysically, it is seen to be the "Great Balancer," balancing the heart chakra, affecting the circulation, and thus the rest of the body by way of the circulation of blood and energies. I do not believe that gold necessarily must be ingested physically in order to be of value, or to be worked with on an inner level. In other words, don't run to your nearest vitamin store looking for "gold supplements," unless you are recommended to do so by a competent health practitioner. Working with gold jewelry

Table of Planetary Metals

PLANET	METAL
Sun	gold
Moon	silver
Mercury	mercury
Venus	copper
Mars	iron
Jupiter	tin
Saturn	lead

magically (as a talisman or amulet), or even just wearing it with consciousness and intention, should help you become attuned to the energy of gold.

FIRE PRACTICES

FIRE ALTARS

I love to build Fire altars. I find myself building and using them when I'm feeling a lack of spark and passion in my life, and thus a desire to get things ablaze. Here are some ideas for you to use.

Fire Element (pure and simple)

Begin with a simple altar; add a red-gold altar cloth to represent the color of the fire itself and a small figurine of a Salamander to represent the Elemental spirit of Fire. Dragon and/or snake figures usually find their way onto this altar too. I accent the basic altar cloth with smaller pieces of cloth of other fire-related colors and place a group of votive candles on it in the shape of a circle. In the center of the candle-circle I place a larger candle and lean against it a small, gold ceramic sun figurine. The magical tool for Fire, the wand, can also be placed on the altar. Sunlike flowers, such as small sunflowers, chamomile, and calendula, add a beautiful touch, as do rubies, garnets, volcanic rocks, bloodstone, and other stones with Fire associations.

In addition, sun-associated herbs may be used, chosen with regard to the magical work you wish to do or the specifics of what you are trying to represent with the altar. (Consult a book on magical herbalism such as *Mastering Herbalism* by Paul Beyerl, or any of Scott Cunningham's herb books. See Suggested Readings.) Representations of gods and goddesses associated with the Element of Fire, such as Brigid, Pele, or Lugh, may be used, as may pictures of fires, erupting volcanoes, the Sun, and the stars. Tarot cards such as the Sun, the Star, and the King or Queen of Wands may also be used. Dragon's blood may be used as an incense.

Fire Season/Summer

Decorate your altar as above, but keyed to Summer with the addition of seasonal items such as summer flowers and fruits. I usually find ways to represent the astrological signs of Summer by creating the shape of their glyphs with stones. Or, try creating a Sun-shaped pattern, complete with rays, with red/orange/gold stones.

Here is a meditation to help you get in touch with the fire within you. It helps if you can read it into a tape recorder to play for yourself later on, thus allowing you to close your eyes and sink deeply into an altered state while you experience it.

FIRE ELEMENT MEDITATION

PREPARATION

If you have a fireplace, light a fire within it, turn off the lights and sit in front of your hearth. Place several lighted candles around the room. If you do not have a fireplace, create a circle of candles as a stand-in for a fireplace. As you light the candles (and hearthflame), think about the fire of the Sun, about the hearthfire, and about fire of the candle flame.

If you desire to do this meditation in a formal ritual space, the area should be decorated in Fire colors and motifs. Cloths of red, orange, and gold may used for altar cloths and wall hangings. Some images of salamanders and/or dragons/serpents should be present. Decorate with candles, lava rock, and other Fire correspondences. Tarot cards from the Suit of Rods/Spears may also be used, if desired. When all is ready, the meditation may be begun by casting a circle, if desired.

INDUCTION

Make yourself comfortable. Close your eyes, take a deep breath, and relax. Continue to breathe slowly and deeply and feel yourself getting more and more relaxed and comfortable. With each breath you take in, you feel yourself becoming more relaxed; with each breath you breathe out, you feel yourself letting go of the cares and concerns of the day, breathing out what is no longer needed. Feel your body as you sit wherever it is that you are comfortably sitting. As you breathe slowly and deeply, become aware of how your own energy feels. Continue to breathe slowly as you allow your mind to calm itself and to grow clear and still.

FIRE MEDITATION

Imagine yourself growing roots, and sinking them down into the Mother Earth; allow them to sink down and down, through layer after layer, till they reach Her fiery, molten core. Anchor your roots in this molten core, grounding yourself here. Draw this molten, fiery energy into yourself through your roots. Then become aware of your heart beating. Feel this for a few moments; visualize your blood as it is pumped through your heart and feel it circulating within your veins, vessels, and arteries. (PAUSE) Feel into your solar plexus and imagine the process of nutrient separation and absorption going on inside of you. Feel warmed and nourished. You have found the physical fires within you.

As you continue to breathe slowly and deeply, allow yourself to become more and more deeply relaxed. Allow your body to become completely comfortable and your mind to become still. Sit for a few moments and breathe quietly, slowly, deeply, allowing this to happen. (PAUSE)

As you relax and become aware of your body comfortably resting here, become aware of the fire burning in the fireplace before you. Feel the warmth that it radiates and listen for a few moments to the crackle of the flames. Think about the hearthfire and how it warms all those who sit around it, and unites them in this way. (PAUSE) Become aware also of the candles burning around the room, silently, for the most part, giving out their light, heat, and beauty.

Think about the Moon outside in the night sky, shining with her beautiful, silvery, cool light. But of course we know she shines by reflecting the light of the Sun, so now let us think about the Sun for a few moments. Allow yourself to conjure up in your imagination what it feels like to be sitting outside on a warm, sunny day. See the dazzling brilliance of the Sunlight as you feel its warmth bathing your body, penetrating your skin, and going deeply inside of you, warming you. (PAUSE)

As you sit here, warm and comfortable, feel how your roots extend deep into the Earth, into the molten core, the fiery heart of the Earth, the realm of Brigit Begoibne. Feel how you are fed through these roots, breathing Brigit's fiery/earth energy up into your body. Feel how it nourishes you, warms and vitalizes you. Feel also how you are connected to the Sun and stars, through the energy conduit that spirals up from your crown chakra to these places. Allow yourself to become aware of this particular connection, and feel how the solar and stellar energies shower down upon you, and likewise feed and nourish you. (PAUSE)

Having been fed by all these fires, allow yourself now to be conscious of what it feels like inside of you. Reach inside yourself and find the places that are Fire. Become aware of your heart, your solar plexus, and all the space and places in between. This is your center, your Sun center. Feel this. This is your personal hearthfire. Feel the fire that burns here. Feel what goes on here. (PAUSE) From your solar plexus many nerves radiate outward, carrying messages all throughout the body. Part of your digestive process occurs in here—nutrients are absorbed and pass into your bloodstream. From your heart, blood is pumped out, carrying oxygen and nutrients to all areas of your body, and blood is received back into your heart to be sent to the lungs for reoxygenation. From your heart, heartstrings of love radiate outward, as you connect with your fellow beings. Feel the energy as it circulates here, spinning, spiraling through your chakras, centering here. Feel how the fire brought up through your roots from the heart of the earth burns here. Feel how the Sun radiates here. Feel how the Galactic Central

SunFire, spiraling down through your crown, showers down into you and coalesces here, feeding you. (PAUSE) This is your Hearthfire, your heartfire. Feel it, bask in it, as it warms and sustains you.

Breathe with this. Breathe all the fires that are outside of you into you; and feel the union between them all. Become Fire—flicker, leap, glow.

Bringing this awareness with you, now begin to return to normal consciousness. You are centered in your heart/hearth. Continue to remain centered there as you allow yourself to become more aware of your surroundings. Allow your breathing to return to normal and when you are ready you may open your eyes.

FIRE EXERCISES

1. In a darkened room, light a candle and sit before it. (This exercise may also be done sitting with your Hearthfire.) Look at it, noticing every aspect of it. Watch the dance of the flame, the color of it, the slight, occasional hissing sound, the drip of wax as the candle melts. Move your hand close enough to feel the heat coming from this small flame. Notice how much light one candle brings into the dark room, and the shadows that are cast. Once again, look at the flame of the candle. Breathe calmly, slowly, deeply, and allow your inner sense to begin moving and dancing with the flame of the candle. Become one with the warmth of the candle's flame. Now imagine yourself as a flame, golden orange, flickering, dancing. Allow your consciousness to merge with the flame. Stay with this, experiencing it, for several moments, then return yourself to your normal consciousness.

2. Try Fire-Scrying: In a darkened room, sit before your fireplace or before a large, lighted candle. Breathe slowly and quietly, allowing yourself to become calm as you gaze steadily, easily at the fire. Watch the patterns made by the flickering, dancing flames (maybe you will see a Salamander!). Notice the pictures that are to be seen in the glowing embers. Allow yourself to become slightly "hypnotized" by this phenomena, and allow your vision to "fuzz" over slightly as you open yourself to any impressions you might receive. When you feel complete, give thanks to the fire, close your eyes for a few moments, and take three deep breaths with the intention of returning to normal consciousness. Then open your eyes again.

3. Realizing that Fire purification is often the most drastic purification of the Four Elements, think of an aspect of your life that you would like to have purified by Fire. In a ritual setting, write it down on a small piece of paper. Then pray to the Powers of Fire and ask them to take this aspect, to purify and transmute it. Feed the paper to the flames, either by casting it into your fireplace, or by burning it in a small fireproof container. Thank the Fire spirits for taking care of this for you.

4. Get up some morning before sunrise and go outside. Face the direction of the rising Sun and watch it as it rises. Greet the Sun as a relative: Grandfather/Grandmother Sun (your preference, it varies from culture to culture). Greet the Sun by one of the many names used by your ancestors for the Sun God/Goddess. Give thanks for the new day that is dawning and ask for the blessings of Grandfather/Grandmother Sun. Ask for healing on whatever in your life needs healing. Acknowledge your relationship with the Sun; remember, its fires burn within you. Try to really *feel* this relationship.

5. At sunset, turn towards the setting Sun and bid it farewell, thanking it for the gift of this day. Once again, acknowledge the Sun as a relation, calling it by one of its old names. Give thanks also for the beauty of the sunset. Feel the nourishment this beauty brings to you.

6. Develop a habit of awareness and thankfulness toward Fire. Each time you strike a match, light a candle or hearthfire, each time you turn on a burner under a pot of food, take a moment to be aware of the gifts of the Fire Element. Keep a votive candle in a small, sand- or earth-filled bowl in your kitchen. Take a moment to light this candle before you begin meal preparations, thinking lovingly of those who will be partaking of the food you are about to cook, thanking the Powers of Fire for the assistance they will be rendering to you, and offering the gift of your work to the Powers of Life.

7. Go to an area where it is safe to build a fire, and build a bonfire. As we have learned, to our ancestors it was known as a "bone-fire" because bones were used as part of the fuel, a giving back to the Gods of some of the very marrow of life. Build your bonfire; sit before it and use your imagination to take you back to another time when the whole village would be sitting with you around a ceremonial bone-fire. Make an offering to the fire (cornmeal, tobacco, or some dried herbs) and give thanks to it. Appreciate the beneficence of Fire, at the same time you are keeping a wary eye out for stray sparks. Thus you are reminded of the neutral nature and the immense power of Fire. Let respect for Fire grow in your heart as you sit before it. When you are finished, give thanks again, and make sure your fire is completed and thoroughly extinguished before you depart.

8. When you are feeling in need of inspiration, make a special altar to Brigit, the Goddess of Inspiration. Use fire-colored cloths and candles and a Brigit's Cross to represent Brigit. Realize that as Goddess of Inspiration she partakes of all the Elements, but especially Fire and Air. The particular power of Inspiration we are referring to here is that of the power of Air feeding and enabling Fire. Sit before the altar and light the candles. Pray to Brigit and ask her to grant you Her help and inspiration. Sit before the candle, gazing at the flame and as you breathe, feel

yourself filling with Fire. Feel this fire as the Fire of Inspiration. As you breathe in and out, in and out, feel yourself filled with more and more Inspiration, until you are so totally filled with the Fire of Inspiration that you are one with it.

9. Compose an invocation to the Powers of the Fire Element. Work with what you have learned and discovered about the nature of this element and work at reducing it into a few relevant and personally meaningful words. Write it in poetic form if you like, or even in the form of a song or chant. Make it short and simple enough to be easily committed to memory, and let it reflect your personal feelings of appreciation and love for the Element.

10. Ask yourself the following questions:

• What things in my life are blossoming and growing?

• What things in my life are becoming beautiful, bringing joy or satisfaction, even though they may require hard work?

• What in my life is "showing me the light," allowing me to see things more clearly, bringing me "enlightenment?" How does this feel?

• If I try to consider all of this as if soaring over it all like an eagle, does a pattern present itself to me? Does the overview provide a bigger picture?

SEASONAL MEDITATION: SENSING SUMMER

This is an activity to help you connect with the powers that are flowing through nature at this time of the year: Summertime. According to our calendar, Summertime stretches (in the Northern Hemisphere) from June 21–22, the Summer Solstice, until September 22–23, the Fall Equinox. This is the "official" astronomical timing of the Summer season, beginning on the day of the greatest number of daylight hours, though the Wiccan Wheel of the Year notes Beltane as the beginning of Summer. How and when Summer manifests depends on where you live. In my area of central California, by mid-May it feels like the beginning of Summer. So please use this activity whenever it feels like the right time to do so.

Pick a summer day that is especially beautiful and warm, with blue sky and brilliant sunshine. Find a place in your backyard or in a nearby park where you can be alone and undisturbed for a while. This place should feel like a good place to you, a place that calls to you to come and be there. The place should be full of the lush, full growth of Summer: green grass, brightly colored flowers, fragrant and blossoming herbs, a tree covered with bright summergreen leaves. If you have a garden, or know someone who does, that would be a good place to go in order to be surrounded by the full power of Summer's growth.

When you have found your place stand there for a few moments and settle yourself into it. Close your eyes and take a deep breath, then let it out slowly. Keep breathing slowly as you feel yourself calming down and your energy coming into alignment with the energy of your location. Feel your aura (the energy field around your body) growing and expanding outward to touch all that is around you. Use your imagination to do this; simply imagine a glowing field of light around your body that grows larger or smaller as you wish it to. Picture this in your mind.

In your mind, draw around yourself a golden circle of protective light and thank the God and Goddess for the privilege of being part of such a beautiful planet. Ask the Devas and Nature Spirits to come and be with you and help you appreciate the beauty and wonder of the Earth.

Now open your eyes and look around at everything. Look at the blue sky and any clouds that might be above you, the green Earth beneath you, the growing things around you: grasses, weeds, flowers, herbs, leaves. Look at it all, slowly and carefully, noticing the beautiful, alive colors; noticing the way the light touches everything, the patterns of light and shadow. Look at each thing separately and then at how it looks all together. Just look at it all and drink it into yourself, as if this colorful beauty were a nourishing drink for your soul, as indeed it is. Use your breath and breathe it all into you. Take time doing this, and when you are finished, give thanks for what you have seen, and give thanks for the gift of sight.

Focus now on your sense of smell. Begin sniffing, and noticing what smells and aromas are present. Can you smell the warm, dry aroma of the Earth? Or perhaps the Earth is damp, not dry, and it is a damp earthy smell you are noticing. If you are near the ocean, can you smell the saltiness in the air? If you are near a stream or pond, what scents do you detect from these places? Can you smell the nearby grasses and flowers, the herbs, the trees, or the plants in the garden? Take a slow deep breath now, and smell all these fragrances together. Breathe them into you, allowing them to flow through your whole body with the movement of your breath. Feel yourself being nourished by them. When you are finished, give thanks for what you have smelled, and give thanks for the gift of smell.

Look around for a plant that you know is safe to eat, such as sourgrass, plantain, borage flowers, nasturtium flowers, or dandelion leaf. If you can find nothing you absolutely know to be safe, skip this part of the meditation and go on to the next part. If you find something you know to be safe to nibble, ask the plant's permission to pick just one flower or leaf. Just one. If you get a feeling inside you that the plant is giving you permission to nibble it, say thank you to the plant, send it love, and pick the flower or leaf. Close your eyes now and slowly nibble on the piece of plant, feeling your mouth come alive with the taste sensations. Is it sweet, salty, sour, bitter, spicy? Or does it have a mixture of these tastes? Does it taste good to you? Or not so good? Or maybe just new and unusual? As you continue to chew, feel the taste as it swirls through your mouth. Enjoy the experience, even if the taste is one that you are not used to! You are tasting the life force as it flows through this particular plant being, expressing itself in this particular way. When you have finished tasting, chew and swallow this piece of plant, taking it into you consciously as the holy thing that it is. Give thanks to the plant for sharing itself with you. Give thanks for what you have tasted, and give thanks for the gift of taste.

Now close your eyes again and listen to the sounds of Summer around you. Listen carefully to each and every sound. Are there dogs barking? Are there birds singing, crickets chirping, people talking? Can you hear the wind in the trees, the sound of water flowing, or the soft rustle of plants blowing in a breeze? If you listen very carefully, perhaps can you hear the sap running in the trees, or the sound of the plants growing. Listen, listen to all the sounds around you. Then

separate them out and listen to each sound separately; then listen to them all together again, as if they were an orchestra playing a symphony for you. Drink this into you, these sounds of Summer; breathe them in with your breath. Take your time doing this and when you are finished, give thanks for what you have heard and give thanks for the gift of hearing.

Lie down now upon the ground and begin to feel what is under and around you. First of all, feel yourself as you lie upon the ground. What does your body feel like now? Are you comfortable or not? Cold, hot, or just right? Happy, excited, or calm? Now feel the ground on which you are lying. Is it hard or soft beneath you? Does it feel smooth, grassy, sandy, bumpy, rocky? Is it dry or damp? What does the upper surface of your body, the side of you that is not in contact with the ground, feel like now? Is there a breeze blowing? Can you feel the warmth of the sun as it shines on you? Or are you in the shade, and feeling a comfortable, or perhaps uncomfortable, sense of coolness? Have ants or other little critters discovered you lying there and decided to crawl on you? How does that feel? Let your aura expand very much during this activity. Reach out with your aura, using your imagination to do so, because reaching out with your aura will allow you to feel more. Reach out beneath you now with your aura, so your aura is allowed to sink down into, and feel the Earth. What does the earth slightly below the surface feel like to you when you are feeling it with your aura? Does it feel solid, heavy, slow; or light, quick, and flowing? (PAUSE) Or perhaps something totally different from any of these? Take a few moments to just feel this. (PAUSE) Using your imagination, feel the earth energies as they surge upward from deep inside the earth to show themselves as the vibrant growth and color of Summer. Reach your hands out now and connect with what is around you on the ground. Pick up a rock or twig, run your palms over a patch of grass, finger the stems of a plant, or pull gently on a blade of grass. Let your fingers trace the roughness of a tree trunk or root. Allow yourself to feel this, with both your physical sense of touch and with your energy sensing abilities. If you have done this exercise previously, during another season of the year, notice if things feel any different this time. Drink these sensations into you, breathe them in with your breath, and when you are finished give thanks for what you have felt and sensed, and give thanks for the gift of feeling.

Can you feel how you are part of everything you have seen, tasted, smelled, heard, touched, and felt? (PAUSE) You are part of it all, yet you are your own unique self, too.

Open your eyes now as you lie upon the ground. Be aware of what all your senses are bringing to you. Look up at the sky, then all around, taste the lingering taste of the plant in your mouth, sniff the fragrances and aromas around about you, listen to the sounds surrounding you, feel the Earth beneath you and the energies of the plants and Nature Spirits all around you.

Feel your own energy running inside of you and let it fountain forth from the top of your head, from your hands and feet (don't forget to use your imagination if you need to while doing this). Feed this energy to the world around you. Share yourself with all that has shared itself with you. And once again, give thanks to the trees, the plants, the animals, the wind, the water, and the sky. Give thanks to the bright, warm summer Sun. Give thanks also to the Nature Spirits and the God and Goddess. Tuck this experience safely inside you, to remember forever, and bid the plants and trees farewell with love and gratitude in your heart.

When you feel ready, get up and go home.

CHAPTER FIVE

Water

Water, as a physical substance, is something we use and are familiar with every day of our lives. We drink it, we bathe in it, we wash clothes in it, we can even bend over a puddle of it on a rainy day and see our reflection. If you live near enough to the ocean or other body of water, go outside on a moonlit night and notice how beautifully the moonlight reflects upon it. If you are familiar with Catholicism you know that consecrated water is used ceremonially for blessing and cleansing, just as it is in the Craft. In the Craft the consecrated water we use for these purposes is frequently salted water, thus making it, in one sense, ocean water—amniotic fluid. In the Craft, water is also sometimes used for scrying. We use it as a reflective surface, gazing upon it as a focus to allow our deeper self and its wisdom to emerge, exactly the same way a crystal ball is used.

Though Water can be still and quiet, it is also Water's nature to move, but only when acted on by an outside force of some kind.

If you really reflect on Water's cleansing, blessing, nourishing properties, you will begin to understand how intimately the energy and physical substance that is Water is involved in our lives. If you further consider the still and reflective properties of Water, you will begin to understand Water's mirrorlike quality. If you think about the receptivity of Water, its depth and ability to move, to open and accept things into itself, to ripple, then calm itself, you will begin to get a glimmer of Water's relationship to the realm of emotions.

Interestingly, not only do the foods we eat contain a high percentage of water, but frequently they are cooked in water. Reflect for a moment on the fact that our bodies are about 80–90 percent water, and you will be able to see an even deeper connection with the Water Element. Physically, we are mostly water.

WESTERN MYSTERY TRADITION AND THE WATER ELEMENT

DIRECTION—WEST

The Element of Water is assigned to the Direction of West. The West is the place of dreams and visions, of inner journeys (true also of the North), of introspection, feelings, emotions, and receptivity. According to the Magician's Wheel (page 22), West is a place of *daring*. So there is courage associated with this place on the Wheel: the courage of daring, of risk-taking. Our dreams, feelings, and visions require us to have courage, to take risks, if we are to truly face our dreams and bring them into being, if we truly wish to live with hearts open and emotions flowing. There is an element of receptivity associated with daring. To be daring, one must truly be open to maintaining a come-what-may attitude about life.

The West is also the place of harvest, of fulfillment and decay; it is thus, the place of endings. It takes courage and daring to venture into the darkness of the unknown land, be it the land of death, or the realm of the future. There is mystery in the West, the seeming paradox of dreams and daring, inner and outer, of moving from daytime into dreamtime.

West is the place of the setting Sun, the time of twilight. As we have seen, twilight means *two lights,* neither light nor dark, day nor night. This is traditionally a very magical time of day, akin to being between the worlds. The time of year corresponding to the West is Autumn, which is a time of turning inward after having been very outward. Autumn is about storing the harvest that has been reaped, to sustain you through the Winter just ahead. This time of gathering in is a time of work, but of rest too, and of enjoying the harvest, fruits of your labors. The gradual turning inward brings with it digestion and assimilation of what has gone before. Autumn also is a time of twilight: it is the twilight of the year. The Fall Equinox itself is a day of equal day/equal night, but the year is slipping into darkness, and Fall is the twilight time of the Solar Year. As such, it also, is a very magical time.

The West is the place of our emotions. Emotions flow through us as does Water, the Element of the West. Emotion has been described as energy in motion. If emotions do not flow properly they, like water, are likely to back up, stagnate, and cause illness. To feel is to be alive, to touch life. Life is movement and flow. The Latin root of *emotion* implies movement and a stirring up of something.

MAGICAL TOOL—CUP

The magical tool for the West is the cup or chalice: the cauldron of Cerridwen and of the Dagda, the cauldron of plenty, of regeneration (see Table of Elemental Correspondences, page 18). Cauldrons and cups are vessels which *contain.* What they contain is nourishment, making it easy to see why nourishment, sustenance, and fulfillment are key words associated with the West. From that understanding we can see Water's association with the West. Water is the ultimate sustenance—without it we would all die very quickly. With it we live, and can regenerate and nourish ourselves.

During the time when our physical bodies are forming, we are contained within the cauldron of our mother's womb, bathed constantly in the saline, amniotic waters so similar chemically to the waters of Mother Ocean (this is also true of our blood). We float, swim, and dream in these waters for a space of 10 Moons. These waters cushion us, protecting our small, forming bodies from harm. We are nourished by nutrients that come to us (via the placenta) from our Mother's nutrient-rich blood as it flows through her body. It is said that the Moon rules the tides of the womb just as it rules the tides of Mother Ocean.

The relationship between the Moon and Water/West is worth pursuing here briefly, though it has been well covered in other books. Traditionally in Wicca, we are very attuned to the Moon. We celebrate our Esbats at the Full Moon, it is the Moon Goddess to whom many of our rituals are directed, and we draw down the power of the Moon into the High Priestess during our Full Moon ceremonies—indeed, into all the worshippers. The powers of the Moon overlap with those assigned to the West: reflection, receptivity, emotional sensitivity, psychic sensitivity, intuition, dreaming, nourishment, fulfillment, sharing, the ebb and the flow. These and many more come to mind as we gaze upward at the mysterious, changeable Moon, sometimes appearing like a silver wheel, sometimes as a mirror, sometimes as Diana's bow, sometimes as a moonbowl.

The West is the place of the Mystery of the Tides, the ever changing, rhythmic flow and ebb of the tides of universal power, of which our oceanic tides are physical representation. The tides of Mother Ocean give example of the Magical Principle of Rhythm, which reminds us that just as the tide flows in and out, bringing change, so also do the tides of cosmic power and energy flow in and out, bringing change, active becoming passive,

passive becoming active. This is very closely allied to the Magical Principle of Polarity: Whatever is active and dynamic on the outer planes is passive and latent on the inner planes, and vice versa. These principles bear much thought and meditation, as we contemplate the Element of Water.

Further keywords for the West are giving, sharing, maturity, fulfillment, receptivity, digestion, intuition through receptivity and reflection (as opposed to a more inspiration-type intuition, which is Fire/Air related). It is easy to see how these words relate to the essential harvest and nourishment nature of the West.

ELEMENTAL BEING—UNDINES

The magical Beings/Elemental Spirits associated with the Element of Water are Undines, from the Latin *unda* meaning "a wave." They are sometimes referred to as Nereids (daughters of the Greek sea-god Nereus). They are creatures of the waves, and envisioned as somewhat human in appearance. Sometimes their shapes may be seen in that of waves curling up to crash to the shore, or as faces within the waves. Some picture them as merfolk. As with each of the Elemental Spirits we've looked at here, it is important to remember that these beings are *energies*, and to remain open to whatever form they may choose to assume for you (though there seems to be remarkable agreement about their natures and appearance among those who have made contact with them).

Undines inhabit the waters of the Earth, including *our* waters, physical and emotional. Thus their work is about maintaining the purity and integrity of these waters. Any aspect of Earth or life having to do with flow and feeling is where we will find them. The rhythms of life, the ebb and flow of tides, emotions, ideas; our dreams, our receptivity, our ability to harvest our experiences, to assimilate and be nourished by them, are these all areas where Undines are at work, helping us develop and maintain healthy emotional bodies,

helping things flow, and stay in correct rhythm. As you can see, this covers a lot of territory.

DREAMING

West is the place of dreams and dreaming, and considering the fact that we spend about half of our lives asleep (averaging in babyhood and elder years), and much of this time dreaming, this very important aspect of our lives merits some discussion in this chapter on Water/West. The past century has seen much research in dreams and dreaming, and many theories have arisen about the hows, whys, and whats of our dreaming life. Everything from conflict, to repressed sexual or other impulses, to random neurological activity has been suggested as the cause of dreams. Everything from great profundity to utter meaninglessness has been suggested as to the meaning and relevance of dreams. Many books have been written on all aspects of dreaming, especially the meaning of the various symbols in our dreams. What I offer you here are my own personal dream theories and strategies, based on my own experiences with my own dreams. My hope is that these experiences will inspire you with ways to work with the magic and meaning in your own dreams.

By adolescence I had begun to realize that some of my dreams were prophetic, though I did not use that word. I just knew that, in addition to the *déjà vu* experiences that we all have (which seemed to happen to me quite often), I had dreams which foreshadowed things to come. This was not a pleasant experience, as more than one of these dreams had to do with a family member's death. By my mid-teens I was having recurring dreams that I finally determined were past life remembrances. These were not pleasant either, and usually were about scenes leading up to my death in that particular life. When I finally figured out these were past life memories, I was able to come to some degree of peace and resolution about them, and they stopped.

In the early days of my magical training, it was suggested to me that I keep a dream journal. This was a difficult undertaking, since I had a small, nursling baby at the time, and when babies awaken to be fed, they care not the slightest bit about your need to make an entry in your dream journal! I wrestled with this problem for a while, till solutions finally began to emerge. Over time, I worked these various solutions into a strategy that was very helpful to me, and which has often proved helpful for others.

The years of journaling and working with my dreams have shown me that there are several types of dreams. The first type is what I call the Garbage Dream. This type really does seem to be a sort of random, strange, misfiring of neurological impulses, composed of experiences and feelings you've had within the last few days or weeks. Wishes and fears may surface here, but the disconnected, random quality to these dreams make it impossible to really take them seriously. Occasionally there will be something of value to be picked out of this mess, but not too often. When I notice myself having these kinds of dreams, I realize my mind is doing housecleaning, picking things up, shaking them out, throwing them out in no particular order. Sometimes I try to link up the various pieces with the relevant pieces of my waking life, but I try not to take too long on this.

The second kind of dream is what I call a Physiological Dream. Sometimes my body is trying hard to tell me something, and the only way it can get through to me is in my dreams. I've received dreams that made me realize I needed to go to the dentist, or that I needed to amend my diet in a particular way. Sometimes I dream about a particular food I need to eat. When I wake up and think about it, it inevitably proves to be the very thing that addresses an imbalance I'm suffering at that moment. These dreams, though they make me smile, always make me feel really *dense*, since they make me realize I'm not paying attention to body messages the way I should.

The third kind of dream is what I call a Psychological Dream. In these dreams I find that I'm working really hard on some problem or situation of my life, and my mind has used dreams to bring forth various pieces of insight for my consideration. Sometimes these are insights into the dynamics of the situation itself. But frequently, these are insights into my own emotional and psychological processes. I awaken, able to understand certain of thoughts/reactions in my current life situations as having arisen from emotional states or mental structures, of which I was previously unaware, or to which I was just not owning up.

It has been stated by some dream experts that every dream is about the dreamer and that every person, place, or thing in the dream in some way represents the dreamer. But my dream experiences have taught me otherwise. Most dreams may perhaps be that way, but the fourth kind of dream in my system of classification is what I have come to call a Mystical Dream. These dreams are very different in both content and feeling from those of the preceding categories. This is where I place past-life memory dreams, though there may be a crossover of categories here, since it could be said that these fit also into the category of Psychological Dreams. This is true in the sense that sometimes the emotional and thinking patterns shown in these dreams are patterns carried over from previous lives. Mystical dreams are sometimes akin to visions, and though they may have relevance to my personal life, usually there is a transpersonal aspect to them. Prophetic dreams definitely fall within this category, as do dreams I call Big Dreams. These are the ones that contain so much information and insight on so many levels (only one of which is personal), and are often so prophetic on a very transpersonal level, that I spend days and months working them out. I don't know if everyone has dreams like this, but I suspect that most people do. Frequently I feel these dreams are to be shared, since they contain material that is not just relevant to my own life. Often I refer to these Big Dreams as Medicine

Dreams, since I am greatly empowered by the revelations, insights, and guidance.

Understanding dreams requires learning their language, which is the language of symbolism. Though there are some symbols that may be considered to be universal, I feel that each of us needs to come to an understanding of our own, unique, dream symbolism. This is only done by paying attention to our dreams, recording them, thinking about them, and asking for understanding of them. If we do this, a personal, unique, symbolic language emerges for us.

The first step toward working with dreams is to remember them long enough to write them down in a dream journal. Here are some techniques for doing that.

Dream Capturing

Do not open your eyes immediately upon awakening. Allow your mind to retain that last dream picture, and notice your emotions. Ever so gently, touch back into that emotional state and try to travel backwards in the emotion to see why you are feeling that way. Force nothing, simply *allow*. After a while, more pictures from the dream will float into your head, and more feelings. Give yourself permission to open your eyes without losing any of this information. Write down those feelings and pictures. After many days of doing this, you will get a lot of information, and find you are able to travel further and further back into your dreams.

Key Words

Being unable to write it all down at once due to the needs of small, mobile children, necessity mothered the invention of another technique. I began attaching *key words* to certain parts of the dream, and suggesting to myself that when I was free to do my dream work, consciously bringing that key word to my mind would bring back that segment of the dream to me, so that I could write it down. In time, this technique worked so well that I found I was writing reams of information on

each dream, far more than I really wanted or needed. I began recalling every tiny aspect, detail, nuance, and feeling of every dream. I found I was following the dream-thread back through four or five dreams. Months of dutifully recording all this taught me to feel out the parts that were most valuable, and record only these. This took a while to learn, since sometimes a small, simple detail of a dream can be the key to something much bigger. The feeling quality of a thing is often the key to it.

Intuitive Hits

I learned early on to pay attention to any interpretation of the dream that came to me immediately and without analysis. I found these unsolicited, intuitive "hits" to be extremely accurate. Later on, I learned that sometimes by simply asking for more information as to the meaning of a dream, I was given it. This works best if you ask right after waking, as soon as you're aware of having had a dream and know you need help in understanding it. I've also found this works best with Mystical Dreams, though it does work with the other types also.

Dreams are a fascinating portal into our inner selves and into other realms of consciousness, and can be a wealth of insight and wisdom. These riches of our nightlife are potential treasures, and should not be ignored. Sleeping and dreaming are important, otherwise, we wouldn't be designed to spend so much time engaged in these activities!

We live in times of great, significant change. We are on the brink of the Age of Aquarius. Our dreams offer us the means of linking into deep levels of these changes, and our accompanying inner changes and transformations, and offer assistance in knowing how to move with the changes.

TRADITIONAL CHINESE MEDICINE AND THE WATER ELEMENT

Think for a moment about the physiological functions of water and fluids within our bodies. In

TCM, the Water Element is connected with the Kidney/Bladder Meridians for obvious reasons. In Western esotericism Water is connected with the second chakra, and therefore with bodily functions having to do with liquid: circulation, urination, reproduction; as well as with emotions: sexuality, sensation (feelings and feeling), and nurturance.

But what does all this mean? It means, for one thing, that we have tremendous self-healing abilities, because as stated in the beginning of this chapter, we have within us the abilities to cleanse, to nourish, to reflect and to bless both ourselves and others. Looked at another way, as the Water within moves through our bodies, it is constantly (and usually we are unconscious of this fact) cleansing and nourishing our cells. If we use this cleansing/nourishing energy in a conscious manner, we then can utilize the other qualities of Water which allow us to feel and reflect on our emotions, and to bless. Cleansing, blessing, and nourishing are all related, one flowing out of the other and into the next.

CHAKRAS AND THE WATER ELEMENT

All systems of Element/chakra correspondence I have studied relate the Water Element to the second chakra. As the second chakra is the place of creativity, the womb, and water-related functions in general, it is easy to see why this is so.

WATER CORRESPONDENCES

Colors associated with the West and with Water are the watery colors: the blues, greens, and silvery grays of Mother Ocean; the special green of rivers, the indigo-blue of a sky just past sunset, and the gleaming silver of the Moon.

Planets associated with the Water Element are the Moon (mentioned above and ruling the water sign of Cancer) and Neptune (astrologically, ruler of the water sign of Pisces and mythologically, considered to be the ruler of the seas).

Herbs associated with the Element of Water are those ruled by the watery Moon: willow, chickweed, iris, lettuce, cleavers, poppy, cucumber, lily (Moon); in addition, the seaweeds (incredibly nutritious, mineral rich, and blood building) are here, as is watercress, which grows in streams (though it is quite spicy, thus may be better used to represent a weaving together of two or more Elements, Water and Fire in this case).

Stones associated with the Water Element are sandstone from the beach, seashells, moonstones, pearls, and stones with cool, blue, and watery hues, such as the beautiful aquamarine. The metal, silver, of course, has long been associated with the Moon, and thus with the Water Element.

WATER PRACTICES

WATER ALTARS
Water Element

When I want to create an altar that is just Water, I consider the many moods and sources of Water. If I need something representing Mother Ocean's waters (I live near the ocean, thus most of my Water altars reflect this fact), I use a blue, blue-green, blue-gray, or silvery altar cloth, with a white scarf representing sea foam. I decorate it with seashells, seaweed, and representations of fish and other sea creatures. My desire is to create a feeling of ebb and flow—as the tides ebb and flow, so do our emotional states. When I want an altar to represent Water with more layers of symbolism, I use a cauldron, chalice or bowl of water, with seashells and seaweed nearby, perhaps sitting on a small blue scarf. Sometimes I set the Queen of Cups Tarot card on the altar too, as she is the prime symbol of the Feminine power of Water in the Tarot. I try, in some way, to represent the merfolk. If possible, I fill my chalice or cauldron with sea water; if not I add sea salt to the water during the circle casting so that the water "becomes" sea water, the primal womb of life on this planet. Sometimes though, it is not Mother Ocean's symbolism that I want or need on my altar. Sometimes I may choose to represent a river, a well, a spring, a lake, or other water source. A brown-green cloth representing Earth is placed on my altar. A bluish-green chiffon cloth becomes a river, a round mirror becomes a well. I also keep handy postcard-sized pictures of holy wells such as Glastonbury Well, rivers, and lakes for use on my altar. Pictures or other representations of water-dwelling creatures can add to the effect.

Water Season/Autumn

Autumn altars made to reflect both Autumn and Water symbolism are going to be different than those made simply to reflect the season of Autumn. In this case the waters of Autumn, the rains, are represented on my altar in the form of pictures and symbols, as are the Thunderbeings.

I'll never forget an incredible lightning storm I witnessed over the sea last year just at the moment of the Fall Equinox. Since then, I have always wanted to remember the Thunderbeings and the lightning bolt on my Autumn altars. Water-colored altar cloths can be decorated with plants symbolic of the season of harvest/thanksgiving such as apples, grains, corn, pumpkins, etc., as well as with seaweeds, nourishing harvest of Mother Ocean. Altar cloths of the harvest colors of brown, gold, and orange may be used. A cauldron, symbolic of the powers of both water and sustenance, is always appropriate.

Here is a meditation to help you connect with the element of Water. It helps if you can read it into a tape recorder to play for yourself later on, thus allowing you to close your eyes and sink deeply into an altered state while you experience it.

WATER ELEMENT MEDITATION

PREPARATION

If you desire to do this meditation in a formal, ritual space, the area should be decorated with water colors and motifs. Cloths of blue, sea, or river green should be used for the altar and for wall hangings. Some representation of sea creatures (or fresh water creatures) should be present: pictures or statues of fishes, dolphins, whales, and merfolk. Dried seaweed (available in most natural food stores) and seashells could be used on the altar. If desiring a "fresh water" altar, use river rocks and plants as part of your decor. A vessel of water, fresh or salted, should be on the altar. Tarot cards from the Suit of Cups may be used, if desired. When all is in readiness, cast a circle, and begin.

INDUCTION

Take a deep breath and relax. Let it out, slowly, and take another deep breath. Feel yourself calming, quieting, as you continue to breathe slowly and deeply. Allow yourself to become still, quiet, comfortable, and relaxed, and continue to breathe slowly and deeply.

WATER MEDITATION

Picture in your mind the ocean. See it clearly: the white-capped breakers against the green gray of the waves, against the blue of the sky. Hear the sound of the waves crashing to the shore, smell the saltiness of the sea, feel the touch of it on your skin as if you had immersed your hand in it. Imagine yourself tasting this ocean water now, just a sip of its saltiness from your cupped hands. Sprinkle some drops of this salty sea water over you (PAUSE); notice how it feels on your skin. Savor these sensations for a few moments. (PAUSE) Think now of the beings who live in this water, the Undines. Send them love and gratitude for their friendship and their beauty. (PAUSE)

Now picture in your mind a lake at sunset: calm, clear, blue-green, its surface a mirror for the sky above and the trees surrounding it. Notice how the colors in the sky made by the setting Sun reflect in this lake. Step into the lake, wade out a bit, then turn over and float, allowing yourself to be borne up, supported, and carried by the water of this lake. Be with these images for a few moments. (PAUSE) Remember the Undines who live in this water. Send them your love and gratitude for their beauty and assistance.

Now picture in your mind a rushing river, tumbling past you as you stand on its banks; this river is rushing and tumbling over rocks in its path, carrying bits of leaf and wood as it flows down the mountainside to its ultimate destination of the sea. Put your hands into this water and feel how cold and refreshing it is. Feel how fast the water is moving as it swirls and rushes past your hands. Feel the power of this rushing, flowing water as it pulls on your hands, nearly tugging you off balance. Spend a few moments experiencing these things. (PAUSE) Be aware of the Water Beings who live in this water. Send them love and gratitude for their beauty, grace, and power.

Reach inside of yourself now, feel into your body, feel into your cells, your psyche, your emotions. Find where you are water. Feel this water within you, the fluidity, the movement, the flowing part of your nature. Feel your emotions; know the heights and depths you are capable of experiencing emotionally. (PAUSE) Realize that the Water Beings, the Undines, live also within you, in the watery part of you. Send love and gratitude to this water within you and to these Undines for the many jobs they do, and for the love they have for you.

As you feel the water within yourself, reach out and pick up the glass of water that is in front of you.

Let this water represent all the waters that are outside of you. Spend a moment blessing this water and thanking it. Now drink it. Receive it consciously into your body. Be aware that you are drinking in the Water Beings who live within it, as you unite the outer waters with your inner waters. Feel your union with the Element of Water. *You are Water.* Flow along now, as you travel your watery pathways, and realize that in the act of flowing you are carried to the heart of the Great Mystery. (PAUSE)

Continue to remain centered in this realization as you allow yourself to become more aware of your surroundings. Allow your breathing to return to normal and when you are ready you may open your eyes.

WATER EXERCISES

1. Use your morning or evening shower as a sacred cleansing ritual. Greet your Brothers and Sisters of the Water. Thank them for allowing themselves to be channeled through the pipes and into your home. Make it your intention that you will allow yourself to be cleansed and purified by this water, and repeat this intention again as you feel the water spraying over your body. Visualize all parts of this process, in a very conscious, respectful manner.

2. This exercise can be done in a bathtub or hot tub. If doing it in a bathtub, fill the tub with comfortably hot water. Get into the tub. Allow yourself to relax and get very comfortable. Become very aware of the warm water surrounding and enveloping you, and the pleasurable feeling of it touching your skin. Allow your hand (or foot) to float freely in the water. As you watch and feel it, become aware of the supportive, buoyant quality of water. Raise it slightly above the water level, then slide it gently back into the water and notice how this feels. Lift your hand again but this time allow it to fall back with a splash. Watch the droplets of water as they splash and move through the air and come down again. Swirl your hand through the water and notice how it moves, then lift your hand out and watch the movement till it subsides. Think about this and what it teaches you about water. Lie within the comforting cocoon of the hot water and visualize yourself as an embryo, floating within your mother's womb. If possible, dunk your head under water for a few seconds and notice how different things sound. Listen to the sounds of your own body from this perspective.

3. This exercise can be done as part of the tub exercise, or on its own. With your body immersed in water, imagine that as you breathe you are breathing in water instead of air, and that this is perfectly comfortable and normal. As you breathe, breathe not only with your lungs, but with every pore on your body, so that you are filling yourself totally with water. In this way, you gradually *become* water. Enjoy this feeling for a few minutes, and notice how it feels. Notice any special sensations or revelations that may come to you (perhaps you may make contact with the Undines in this way). Then gradually imagine any "excess" water you may have (remembering that the human body is 80–90 percent water normally) being emptied from you, flowing from your every pore. When you are done, return yourself to normal consciousness.

4. Here is a variation on the last exercise. As you sit immersed in water, filling yourself with water, becoming water, feeling yourself to *be* water, allow yourself to be open to impressions, and send out a question: e.g., Where is Aunt Sara? What's happening now with Cousin Paul? Be perfectly open and receptive to whatever impressions and pictures you receive as a result of doing this. Later on try to find out how accurate your intuitive impressions were.

5. Here is another variation on the tub exercise. Before you get into your bathtub, take a few grains of sea salt between your fingers and

bless it. Then cast it into the water and ask blessing on the water. The salt, in addition to being representative of the Earth Element, is a crystalline substance, and thus has the amplifying power of crystal. It will amplify the blessing you put into it and into the water. Then take what is called a Lustral Bath, wherein your intention is, in a very sacred manner, to cleanse and purify body and soul. As you lie in the bath, visualize all that troubles you flowing out of your body and soul and into the bath water. Thank the water for receiving these from you. If you have a shower in your tub, rinse off briefly and get out. As you dry off, watch your troubles and other impurities going down the drain. Know that they will be dissolved and, on an energetic level, returned to their primal, pure state. Lustral baths are good to do before ceremonies and also just when you feel a need for them. They may be further enhanced by the use of carefully chosen herbs.

6. If you live near Mother Ocean, go down to the shore and watch the waves for a while. Allow your mind to become empty, and allow yourself to absorb and feel the rhythms of the surf as it ebbs and flows. Become one with this rhythm. After a while, return to normal consciousness; then remember the moods and rhythms you have witnessed, and try to see the connection between them and how your emotional states ebb and flow. If you wish, go swimming in Mother Ocean and experience the rhythm of the waves firsthand, allowing yourself to be mindfully carried back to shore on the waves. Be cautious, and don't let yourself get further out than your swimming abilities are capable of handling.

7. Practice scrying with water. At a time and in a place where you will be free from distraction, fill a small to medium-sized dark-colored bowl (or black, cast-iron pot) with water. The container should be solid-colored with no spots that might cause distraction. Light a candle and turn out all other lights. Allow your mind to become calm and still. Breathe slowly and evenly as you gaze at the water. Don't stare at it, but soften your gaze (allow it to sort of blur around the edges, or gaze beyond the surface of the water so your focus is not on the surface). Then just be open and receptive to whatever impressions might come to you. Don't be disappointed if nothing does; this one takes a bit of practice for most people.

8. Practice Sacred Clothes Washing. As you consign your dirty clothing to the washing machine, ask the water and Water Spirits to dissolve and remove not only the physical dirt and stains on the clothes, but also the subtle dirt—whatever energies have accumulated on the clothing during your wearing of it that need to be cleansed and removed. Give thanks for this.

9. Develop a good habit: each time you reach for a glass of water (or any beverage) to drink, stop for a few seconds and become aware, in the manner indicated in the "Water Meditation" (pages 97-98), of the *Water Within*. As you drink the water be aware of the Water Beings living within the water you are drinking. Also be aware of how the water is nourishing and moistening your body, providing the moisture that is vital to life. Practice doing this daily for a week, or till a second or two of very conscious awareness of this automatically precedes every glass of water you drink.

10. When you are feeling down and in need of blessing, create this little ceremony for yourself. Consecrate some salt and water, stir them together in your chalice or cup, then ceremonially bless yourself. Use this "holy water" by dabbing or sprinkling it on yourself, *intending* that you be cleansed and blessed by the power of Water. Give thanks for this blessing, and pour the remainder of the water onto the Earth.

11. Compose an invocation to the Powers of the Water Element. Work with what you have learned and discovered about the nature of this Element and work at reducing it into a few relevant and personally meaningful words. Write it in poetic form if you like, or even in the form of a song or chant. Make it short and simple enough to be easily committed to memory, and let it reflect your personal feelings of appreciation and love for the Element.

12. Ask yourself the following questions, and allow yourself to feel the emotions they bring up for you:

   • What things in my life are coming to fullness, or to an ending ?

   • What is ready to be harvested?

   • Which of the fruits of my labors is ready to be feasted upon, digested, assimilated now and during the dark season to come? How does this feel?

   • Am I willing to store some of these harvested experiences, knowledge gained through experience, toward future needs?

   • Am I ready to share some of my harvest with others as appropriate, and perhaps partake of theirs?

Seasonal Meditation: Sensing Autumn

This is an activity to help you connect with the powers that are flowing through nature at this time of year: Autumn. According to our calendar, Autumn stretches from September 23, the Autumn Equinox, until December 21, the Winter Solstice (in the Northern Hemisphere). This is the official astronomical timing of the Fall season—beginning on the day of equal light and dark—though the Wiccan Wheel of the Year notes Lughnasadh as the beginning of Autumn. How Autumn manifests depends on where you live. Where I live, Autumn's presence begins to be felt in mid-September, but is not really in full swing till mid-October. So please use this activity whenever it feels like the right time to do it.

Pick a Fall day that is especially beautiful; a bit chilly, but with blue sky and brilliant sunshine. Pick a day that looks like "Fall" to you, when the deciduous trees have turned beautiful colors and have begun to shed their leaves. Find a place in your backyard or in a nearby park where you can be alone and undisturbed for a while. This place should feel like a good place to you, it should call to you to come and be there. The place should be full of the dying, ending things of Autumn: trees with colorful leaves (if possible where you live), dry grasses and herbs, perhaps the last of the wild berries growing. Perhaps you can even find an area where you can observe squirrels and their kin preparing for Winter with the busy, hoarding wisdom squirrels exhibit this time of year.

When you have found your place, stand there for a few moments and settle yourself into it. Close your eyes and take a deep breath, then let it out slowly. Keep breathing slowly as you feel yourself calming down and your energy coming into alignment with the energy of your location. Feel your aura (the energy field around your body) growing and expanding out to touch all that is around you. Use your imagination to do this—simply imagine a glowing field of light around your body that grows larger or smaller as you wish it to. Picture this in your mind.

In your mind, draw around yourself a golden circle of protective light and thank God and Goddess for the privilege of being part of such a beautiful planet. Ask the Devas and Nature Spirits to come and be with you and help you appreciate the beauty and wonder of the Earth.

Open your eyes now, and look around at everything. Look at the blue sky and clouds above you, the green earth beneath you, the plant beings around you: grasses, weeds, herbs, leaves, and berries. Look at it all slowly and carefully, noticing the beautiful colors and shapes, noticing the way the light touches everything, noticing the patterns of light and shadow. Look at each thing separately and then at how it looks all together. Just look at it all and drink it into yourself, as if this colorful beauty of earth and sky were a nourishing drink for your Soul, as indeed it is. Use your breath and breathe it all into you. Take time doing this, and when you are finished give thanks for the what you have seen, and give thanks for the gift of sight.

Focus now on your sense of smell. Begin sniffing, and noticing what smells and aromas are present. What does Mother Earth smell like this time of year in your region? Is there a dampness from recent rains? Or perhaps the Earth is not damp and it is a drier, earthy smell you are noticing? If you are near the ocean can you smell the saltiness in the air? If you are near a stream or pond what scents do you detect from these places? Can you smell the grasses nearby, or the herbs, or berries, or the trees? Now smell all these fragrances all together and breathe them into you, allowing them to flow through your whole body with the movement of your breath. Feel nourished by them. When you are finished, give thanks for what you have smelled, and give thanks for the gift of smell.

Look around for a plant that you know is safe to eat, such as a wild berry, or perhaps a nut or an apple. Many of the plants are fading away this time of year, so choose one that is alive enough to safely ingest. If you can find nothing you absolutely know to be safe, skip this part of the meditation and go on to the next part. If you find something safe to nibble, ask the plant's (or tree's) permission to pick just one fruit, nut, or leaf; just one. If you get a feeling inside you that the plant is giving you permission to nibble it, say thank you to the plant, send it love, and pick the fruit or leaf. Close your eyes now and slowly nibble on the piece of plant, feeling your mouth come alive with the taste sensations. Is it sweet, salty, sour, bitter, spicy? Or does it have a mixture of these tastes? Does it taste good to you? Or not so good? Or maybe just new and unusual? As you continue to chew, feel the taste as it swirls through your mouth. Enjoy the experience, even if the taste is one that you are not used to! You are tasting the life force as it flows through this particular plant being, expressing itself in this particular way. When you have finished tasting, then chew and swallow this piece of plant, taking it into you as the holy thing that it is. Give thanks to the plant for sharing itself with you. Give thanks for what you have tasted, and give thanks for the gift of taste.

Now close your eyes again and listen to the sounds of Autumn around you. Listen carefully to each and every sound. Are there dogs barking? (PAUSE) Are there birds singing, crickets chirping, people talking? (PAUSE) Can you hear the rustling sound of wind in the trees, the sound of leaves falling, perhaps being crunched by passersby? (PAUSE) Is there water nearby, adding to the symphony, or perhaps the soft rustle of plants blowing in a breeze? (PAUSE) These are just suggestions, though. Listen, listen carefully to all the sounds around you. Then separate them out and listen to each sound separately. Next, listen to them all together again, as if they were an orchestra playing a symphony for you. Drink this into you, these sounds of Autumn; breathe them in with your breath. Take your time doing this and when you are finished, give thanks for what you have heard, and give thanks for the gift of hearing.

Lie down now upon the ground and begin to feel what is under and around you. First of all, feel yourself as you lie upon the ground. What does your body feel like now? Are you comfortable or not? Cold, hot, or just right? Happy, excited, or calm? (PAUSE) Now feel the ground on which you are lying. Is it hard or soft beneath you? Does it feel smooth, grassy, sandy, bumpy, rocky? Is it dry or damp? (PAUSE) What does the upper surface of your body, the side of you that is not in contact with the ground, feel like now? Is there a breeze blowing? Can you feel warmth from the Sun as it shines on you? Or is it a cool day, with a brilliant Sun but no real warmth? Perhaps you are in the shade, and feeling a comfortable, or uncomfortable, sense of coolness. Have ants or other little critters discovered you lying there and decided to crawl on you? Let your aura expand very much during this activity. Reach out with your aura, using your imagination to do so, because reaching out with your aura will allow you to feel more. Reach out beneath you now with your aura, so that part of your aura is allowed to sink down into the Earth and feel it. What does the Earth slightly below the surface feel like to you? Does it feel solid, heavy, and slow, or light, quick, and flowing? (PAUSE) Or perhaps something totally different? (PAUSE) Feel the earth energies as they tuck themselves into the body of Mother Earth in preparation for the winter. Reach your hands out now and connect with what is around you on the ground. Pick up a rock or twig, run your palms over a patch of grass, finger the stems of a plant, pull gently on a blade of grass or caress a fallen leaf. Let your fingers trace the roughness of a tree trunk or root. Allow yourself to feel this, with both your physical sense of touch and with your energy sensing abilities. Drink these sensations into you, breathe them in with your breath. When you are finished give thanks for what you have felt and sensed, and give thanks for the gift of feeling.

Can you feel how you are part of everything you have seen, tasted, smelled, heard, touched, and felt? You are, you know. You are part of it all, yet you are your own unique self, too.

Open your eyes now as you lie upon the ground. Be aware of what all your senses are bringing to you. Look up at the sky, then all around. Taste the lingering taste of the plant in your mouth, sniff the fragrances and aromas around you, listen to the sounds surrounding you, feel the Earth beneath you, and the energies of the plants and Nature Spirits all around you.

Feel your own energy running inside of you and let it fountain forth from the top of your head, from your hands and feet (using the power of your imagination if you need to). Feed it to the world around you. Share yourself with all that has shared itself with you. Once again, give thanks to the trees, the plants, the animals, the wind, the water, and the sky. Give thanks also to the Nature Spirits and God and Goddess. Tuck this experience safely inside you, to remember forever, and bid the plants and trees farewell with love and gratitude in your heart.

When you feel ready, get up and go home.

PART TWO

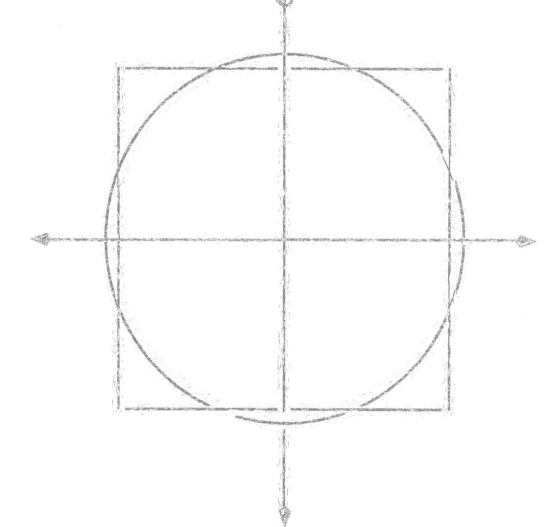

A Weaving of the Elements

CHAPTER SIX

Elemental Weavings

MARRIAGE POINTS

When traveling around the Wheel of the Elemental Powers, one inevitably comes to the place where one element meets and merges with the next on the Wheel. I refer to these places of meeting as the *Marriage Points*. Air merges with (marries) Fire; Fire merges with Water; Water merges with Earth; Earth merges with Air. These are places of great creativity; two Elements merge, and something new—related to both but unique—is produced.

When the power of **Air**—*movement, change, beginnings*—merges with the power of **Fire**—*will, growth, enthusiasm, creativity, passion,* the result is that the movement toward new beginnings is married with the passion, creativity, enthusiasm, and energy necessary for growth and development of what is begun. The result of this union is the power or energy that I have referred to in preceding chapters as the Fires of Inspiration.

When the power of **Fire** is married to the flowing, fertile power of **Water**—*inner dreams and visions, introspection, feelings and emotions, receptivity, nourishment, fulfillment*—then the powers of passion, will, growth, and creativity work together with feelings, receptivity, and nourishment. We are warm and nourished, receptive and creative. Open to the nourishment of our inner dreams, visions, and feelings, warmed by our passion and creative fires, we are enabled to go deeper in our daring—breaking new ground, sending down strong roots, reaching deeper levels of creativity and growth.

When the power of **Water** merges with the *silent, solid, restful, mysterious, wise* power of **Earth**, the power of manifesting structure and form is merged with that which nourishes and blesses its growth. By the power of emotions/feelings it is given depth and vision, receptivity and adaptability, and flow and rhythm. Sensation/sensuality is married to feeling and emotion.

When the *wise, structural, solid* power of **Earth** is married to the *moving and changing* **Air** power, Air's powers of freshness and learning keep things moving—lest Earth's structure/form rigidify and crystallize into something that no longer serves. New ideas are brought into play. Air assures that Earth's wisdom moves outward to the other from the silence. The Mystery is revealed through the power of sound.

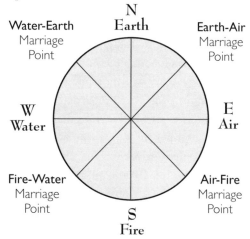

**Wheel of the Elemental
Marriage Points**

How does this manifest within Life, including human life? Sometimes it manifests in very obvious ways; sometimes in less obvious ways. As we have seen, we are all mixtures of the Inner and Outer Elements. Medieval occultists recognized this fact when they spoke of the four human temperaments: Sanguine/Air, Choleric/Fire, Melancholic/Earth, and Phlegmatic/Water, and recognized that though one or two temperaments might dominate a person's nature, each of us contains all of them in some measure. Just as we humans—and our siblings, the animals—are a mixture of these physical and subtle Elements, so also is our world. Our large oceans sit in huge earthen cauldrons. Our rivers race (or meander) through earthen riverbeds, carrying stones and pebbles along with them on their courses. The interaction of the Sun's fire with the fertile, moist earth gives rise to the many plants and trees. Volcanoes steam, then erupt; hot, glowing, molten lava pours forth, solidifying into rock. All life forms (except perhaps anaerobic bacteria) depend on the correct mixture of gases in the air.

We watch the Earth go through her times of wet/dry, hot/cold, expansive/contractive, light/dark, as we go through our own. There is a cycle here, a rhythmic pattern we have named The Seasons. We humans have our own seasons too, and our own internal "weather" (physically, mentally, emotionally, and spiritually). Sometimes it seems as if we go through a whole year's worth of emotional weather conditions in the course of a single day! And it is at the meeting places of our inner Elements that we find the wellsprings of our own creativity and power, not only for *overcoming* challenge and obstacle, but also for *learning* from challenge and obstacle as well. An extreme of one Elemental state may well push us into its opposite. Have you ever wept so much that, finally, it seemed you'd run out of tears, gone from wet to dry? How often do we hear of people who are having physical (health or other) or emotional problems so enormous that the result is some sort of spiritual turnaround? Haven't we all heard of great works of art or music born from life's tumultuous emotional experiences?

It is fairly obvious how "elemental" our emotions can seem: sadness or grief that pierces and penetrates us like the Sword of Air; raging, scorching, consuming, and fiery anger; depression within which we seem to be drowning; smothering fear, which may cause our mouth to go dry, and set the heart to pounding or racing; worry that seems to eat away at our abilities to be grounded (Earth) within the present moment. Anyone with passing acquaintance with Ayurvedic or Chinese medicine will be aware of how intimately connected Elemental balance is with our physical health states. Think about it, and you will also see how we express the Elements on a mental level: excitement (Fire and Air) can make us "high"—can make our minds race. Sometimes our minds feel sluggish, *earthbound*—we just can't get them going. Or occasionally we'll say we feel like our minds are "in a fog" (Water and Air) and we can't see clearly. Of course, mind and emotion are so tied together that it's hard to separate them here, even for the sake of example.

We have our spiritual seasons and weathers and marriage points too. We have times of beginnings, times of "the light dawning," times of growing (often complete with growing pains), times when we realize we've reached a point of maturity, times of fiery enthusiasm, times of wild new spiritual experiences, times when nothing much seems to be happening (yet actually spiritual assimilation is in progress), and times which seem dry, parched, and barren, in need of the waters of nourishment and fertility.

ELEMENTAL PATHWAYS

In addition to the Elemental Weavings at the marriage points, there is another way in which the Elements interact with each other. They form connections by leaping across the circle from side to side. I call these the Elemental Pathways, for they

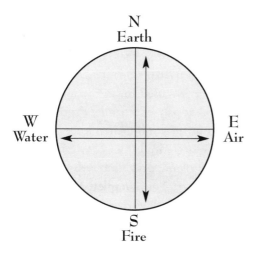

Wheel of the Elemental Pathways

function like pathways that lead to the Center and out again to the opposite Direction.

The Elemental Pathways connect Air to Water (East to West), and Fire to Earth (South to North), and in so doing, move across the point of Center. The connection here is somewhat different in nature from those of the Marriage Points. The power here is that of complementary opposites, opposites that actually empower each other. As these energies reach across the Circle to connect with each other, exchange (giving and receiving) occurs, movement is generated, thus turning the Sacred Wheel of Life. Air/Mind gives to Water/Emotion, and Water gives to Air; Fire/Soul-spirit gives to Earth/ Body, and Earth gives to Fire.

THE TEACHING OF RECIPROCITY

It seems to me that the teaching of these two pathways is the Teaching of Reciprocity. Thus far, we have been speaking of this teaching indirectly; now it is time to speak of it more directly.

What is it that makes the Sacred Wheel of Life turn? No matter what fancy metaphysical concepts we are working with or on, it's really all about energy exchange, or the principle of Reciprocity, often called the Giveaway.

To *reciprocate* is to engage in a mutual exchange of energies: to give and to receive, to make a return for what has been given to one. To reciprocate, to give away, is to recognize oneself to be one with all that is, and yet a Separate Self at the same time—a seeming paradox.

We know that we contain the Elements within us, so in a sense, we *are* Fire, we *are* Water, we *are* Air, we *are* Earth. As we experience what it's like to be all these things, to feel them inside, to feel made of them, we find that as Fire, we flicker, burn, consume, rage; we are passion, we are joy. Sometimes we feel like we are burning out of control, wild with passion and delight, or with consuming rage. As Water we flow, we feel, we receive; we are depth, depth, and more depth. We flow around impediments, we trickle, rush, flood, have tides, and come crashing to shore, then draw out again. Our watery persistence wears away obstacles, weathers them down, dissolves them. As Earth we are solid yet empty, firm yet malleable; deep, silent, alive, fiery at the core, gleaming with crystals inside our body, holding memories in our bones and blood. We endure. We are composed of many beings, and many intelligences. We are aware of them all, in their separativeness, yet also as part of us. We abide. As Air we experience movement of emotions and thoughts, blown by currents that seem to blow in and through us. Winds of change and inspiration whistle through us, bringing freshness, fueling our fires. We breathe, and when we are Air, we become aware of the breathing.

Becoming aware of the breathing, we also become aware that there is a rhythm to all of this. We breathe: in/out, expand/contract. Our finite mind goes in and out of the unitive/separative ways of thinking. This process, in and of itself, feels like a kind of respiration: We breathe in—*I am Earth, Fire, Water, Air* (or perhaps trees, rivers, wind, and stars). We breathe out—*I am a separate Self.* It is in feeling this respiration, particularly on the out-breath, that we begin to feel the significance of "energy exchange." As breath flows out of us, it goes beyond us. If we tune into this, becoming conscious of this rhythm, we cannot help but become aware of "other-than-self." As we continue, inhaling, exhaling, the message we hear is "*receive, yes; but don't forget to give back, give back, give back!*" To do other than this would be like taking in a breath of air, but forgetting the need to breath out, an act necessary to complete the cycle of the exchange of energies/gases. Even the trees must breathe, and perhaps the stars too in their own ways. It is the pulsating, reciprocal rhythm of life we are feeling here.

What does this mean within our lives? The physical act of respiration—breathing in and out—is one thing, and a quite natural, automatic thing at that. But what about other aspects of our life? My feeling is that we must emphasize the teaching of reciprocity, of energy exchange, in our lives. In our lives, in our ceremonies, it's not enough to merely stand before the altar and call upon the powers of the Elements, the Spirit-Keepers, the God and Goddess, and get high off of it. That's just a reworking of the old "taking" mentality again. Better and wiser perhaps, would be for us to change our focus to an awareness of the energy exchange aspect, the reciprocal rhythm of respiration, and find ways to give back to the gods, to spirits, to nature, for what has been given to us.

Life gives to us so abundantly. Spirit gives to us so abundantly. We used to, in the long ago past, *give in return*, as part of a natural process that was ingrained in us on a sub-mental level. We gave of our prayers, our gratitude, our physical wastes, our compost, our blood, and ultimately, of our very bodies themselves. This **completed the cycle** and nourished the Earth. It also nourished our connection with Spirit because it nourished the Earth, and Spirit is one with the Earth. There is no separation.

Putting this into practice in our lives fosters sharing and generosity, cultivates cooperation and appreciation, as well as respect for what has been given. *Respect* comes from the Latin *re* (again) and *spectare* (to look at). When we have respect for something, it is because we have "looked at it again," given it further consideration, and thereby developed an appreciation for it. If we appreciate and respect what we are gifted with by the Divine as well as by the other beings with whom we share the planet, a natural response develops that desire to give back, to reciprocate. In this way the Sacred Wheel of Life keeps turning; all are nourished, and Life continues.

CHAPTER SEVEN

The Magical Winds

As discussed in Chapter Three, one of the qualities of Air is movement. When Air moves we know it as wind. Movement brings change. The winds of change blow through, and things are different because previously existing energy patterns have been altered.

Winds blow in from different directions, and have different qualities arising from the climatic/energetic conditions of their direction of origin. In times past, winds were not only associated with the Directions (referred to in old Scots-Gaelic as the "airts"), but were also given names and associated with Elements. These associations varied from place to place, depending largely on the relative dampness/dryness, and heat/cold brought in by the wind.

People in rural communities, whose livelihood was dependent on good weather for crops and fair winds for fishing, had an incredible number of words describing wind and weather conditions of every conceivable nuance.

Some Traditions separate the concept of the Directions and the Winds, attributing the Winds to the Cross Quarters (known as the intercardinal directions) only. But always and everywhere, the Winds are associated with movement and change.

In an 11th century Irish manuscript known as the *Saltair Na Ran* we find reference to twelve winds, four of which were considered "chief" winds. These winds were named and linked with colors.

- North Wind—*black*
- East Wind—*purple*
- South Wind—*white*
- West Wind—*pale*

Generally speaking, in Ireland the "Black" North Wind was considered to bring misfortune and bad luck. Considering the fiercely cold, destructive, northern winter storms, this is not surprising. The "White" South Wind was beneficial, the bringer of long life and good fortune. The "Dun" West Wind was the wind which was said to 'carry death'. The West was considered the direction of death (and the Otherworlds associated with the afterlife) since this is the direction into which the Sun disappears each night. The "Purple" East Wind was thought to be particularly sacred (purple was a color traditionally reserved for royal usage). East, the direction of sunrise, was said to be the direction from which "no bad influence ever came."

Winds were considered to bring in a variety of influences, so good or evil influences were always flowing through the world, especially when the winds were blowing. It might be an "ill wind" that blew through, bringing in unwanted heat, cold, rain, or pestilence. Or perhaps it was a good wind, bringing in just the right influences at just the right time.

In classical Greek mythology we find reference to the Eight Winds:

- East Wind—*Eurus*
- South Wind—*Notus*
- West Wind—*Zephyrus*
- North Wind—*Boreas*
- Southeast Wind—*Auster* or *Apeliotis*
- Southwest Wind —*Afer* or *Africus*
- Northeast Wind —*Calcius*
- Northwest Wind —*Corus*

The ancient Greeks considered the winds to be important Beings. Their mother was **Eos** (*East*), goddess of Dawn, and their father was the Titan **Astraeus** (from *astron*, meaning *star*). Eos and Astraeus were also said to be the parents of the stars. Thus the winds were considered to be born of the primal, elder powers of Beginnings, and were siblings to the stars—a fair indication of the power attributed to them. The God of the Winds was **Aeolus**; it was said he kept the winds in a cave on his island and loosed them when appropriate.

No wonder the winds were, and are, considered to be magically powerful.

In some of the very old English country traditions of magic, the Four Directions as such are not used at all. Instead, the Four Winds of East, West, South, and North are used. Winds blow, bringing in, as stated above, whatever qualities of heat/cold, wet/dry they carry from their point of origin. This applies magically/symbolically, as well as physically.

Since winds blow, they move energy; thus they were used magically by our magically inclined ancestors to move energy. Invocations were made to the Winds, to bring their specific influences to bear on whatever was the subject of the magical working, and to move the energy toward that end. The Wind thus summoned—carrying the power of its Directional point of origin and its Elemental association—would, by blowing through and onward, carry the power generated by the magical working to its proper destination.

The use of the Four Winds in this magical way was born of the great familiarity with the Winds that comes from living in closer relation to Nature than many of us do these days. A person living in an area where his or her ancestors had resided for a hundred years or more, probably had a deep familiarity with the prevailing winds, their seasons, and their influences, since these had an impact on his or her daily life. Therefore, this magical use of the Winds was simply an extension of his or her everyday relationship with them.

Witches have long been associated with weather magic, in particular the raising of winds. In the records of some of the medieval witch trials, there are accusations against the witches of raising winds and causing storms. In 1662 during a witch trial in Auldearne, Scotland, a witch confessed to this "crime":

> *When we raise the wind we take a rag of cloth and wet it in water, and we take a beetle and knock the rag on a stone and we say thrice over, "I knock this rag upon this stone, to raise the wind in the devil's name. It shall not lie until I please again." (A beetle is a thin, flat, mallet-like piece of wood used for pounding.)*

The North Berwick witches of 1590 were convicted of trying to raise a storm to kill King James VI of Scotland (later James I of England).

In Shakespeare's *MacBeth*, one of the witches plans to stir up a storm to spite a sailor whose wife had annoyed her. Her two sister-witches immediately each offer her a wind, to which she replies:

> *"I myself have all the others; and the very ports they blow, all the quarters that they know, in the shipman's card...."*—Macbeth, Act I, Sc. III

Certain witches on the Isle of Man sold enchanted cords with three knots tied in them to the sailors. When the first knot was untied it brought a good breeze; loosening the second knot caused a strong wind; the third knot's undoing brought a gale force wind.

Similarly, witches were credited with the ability to calm the winds, which was just as crucial as the power to raise them. In an era when winds were necessary to travel by water, and for such tasks as winnowing grain, the ability to raise and calm the winds was a very great power indeed, and one taken quite seriously.

The Druids were seen to be adept at raising winds and storms, creating mists and clouds, as well as sparking terribly destructive fires by use of incantation. "Incantation" has within it the Latin word, *cantare*, meaning "to sing." Incantation is, therefore, song or sound: vibrational frequency-patterns put forth by the power of breath (which is air-in-movement: wind).

Blacksmithing was considered a magical profession, harkening back to the mysterious and magical power of the Artificers—the first Makers—and involving the power and use of the Elements: the Fire of the forge, the Air of the bellows, Earth's gift of iron, and Water for cooling it. So it is not surprising to find that the blacksmith's anvil was considered to be a powerful tool that could be used in spells of raising winds.

These examples show us not only the association of witches and other magical folk with Wind magic, but also give us a clue toward understanding their *magical relationship* to the powers of Air. Witches, and indeed magicians, sorcerers, and shamans in general, have always had the reputation of being able to control/command all of the Elements, and indeed, to have derived much of their power from the Elements.

And since where there is smoke, fire is usually to be found nearby, it is likely this reputation was not completely undeserved, nor unfounded in fact. To be able to "control" an Element, one must be in *relationship* with that Element. One must be able to *become* that Element (in a sense) in order to manifest this seeming power over it. *Becoming* the Element is really *becoming one with* the Element, shifting one's consciousness into a state of merging with the particular Element—more of an attunement process than a power grab. This is not really the same as *controlling* the Element in the same sense that our modern, dominance-oriented culture would define the word. Forget your mental pictures of powerful and glamorous witches and sorcerers, arms upraised, commanding into obedience the powers of lightning, wind, and rain. Try substituting an image of the witch/magician engaged in an intense, inner process of aligning his/her consciousness, intention, and energies with that of the Element and its Governing Intelligence, so that their wills/intentions/actions may be as one, and act as one. For humans to assume they can, merely by the power of their desire and will, overpower and thus control wind, rain, lightning, and other such titanic forces, is a rather amazing demonstration of human ego and hubris. One is reminded of the tale of the Sorcerer's Apprentice.

Because winds blow where they will, they bring much along with them that they have picked up on their travels from place to place. Thus information can be carried on the wind. Many old-time farmers could predict the weather by feeling and tasting the winds that blew through the countryside, as well as by watching the behavior of animals, who likewise sensed change through their instinctual ability to tune into the messages of nature.

Since the winds blow through all the Directions, they partake of (are affected by), to one extent or another, the nature of all of the Elements. Thus they illustrate the Air Element's power to make connections between the different realms. To make these connections is not only to change things, but to open new realms of creativity by the combination of different Elements. Winds are definitely of the Element of Air, but may also be seen to move through and have influence on the other Elemental spheres. Air feeds and keeps alive Fire, combines with Water to create storms, and interacts with Earth to create swirling dust and to blow seeds and spores to their new homes.

Magical use of this important connecting characteristic of the Wind Beings can be of use to us today. Meditate deeply on the magic of the Wind to change things and events by the power of movement and the combination of different Elements. See how this can be of use to you when you want to create change in your life. Get to know the prevailing winds: their temperatures, where they arise, where they are headed, the paths they tend to follow. Play with the breezes that come through. Call to them; see if they respond.

Form a relationship with the Wind Beings to see if they will help you when you are doing magic that involves movement. Do not make the mistake of thinking you can *command* the winds, unless you are prepared to deal with the karmic consequences of gales, tornadoes, and hurricanes should you somehow prove successful. Always relate to them in a very respectful manner, realizing that in calling on them magically you are attempting a co-creative endeavor, and not summoning a slave.

PART THREE

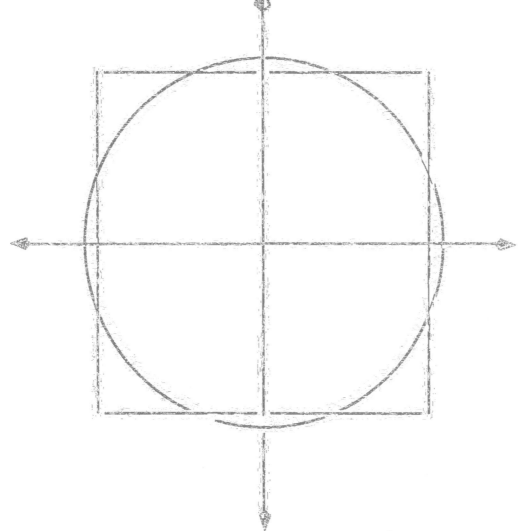

Getting Centered

CHAPTER EIGHT

The Center of the Circle

Gazing into the night sky, our ancestors watched the stars and planets move through their seasonal dances. Over the course of time, they became aware that all the stars of the night sky seemed to pivot around one unchanging point: that which we now refer to as North. Over the vast sweep of the years there was sometimes a star just exactly marking this spot, but sometimes not. It must have seemed that North was, in a sense, the center of the sky circle, since it was the place of stillness in the midst of the great circular round. There is evidence that ancient people used this fixed point as Center, and designated it in several ways.

Indeed, the four cardinal directions derive their meaning from the sky's daily rotation. The fixed Northern point of the sky, around which all else appears to turn, is the primary direction. The other three follow naturally from it.

Astronomical analysis of Medicine Wheels and stone circles throughout the Americas and Europe has shown evidence of alignments with the solstices/equinoxes, with certain stars or groups of stars, with the Moon's "metonic," 18.6 year cycle (the Moon comes into exact alignment with the Sun only once every 18.6 years), as well as many other alignments and correspondences. Ancient astronomies and mythologies bear testimony to the significance of stars or star groupings (such as the Pleiades, Ursa Major, Ursa Minor, Orion) in the spiritual/ceremonial life of many ancient peoples worldwide.

If our ancestors of both Europe and America used the stars to orient and align themselves to the cosmos, as well as to Earth's seasons and cycles, then we of the modern Pagan revival are missing about half of our heritage by tuning in only to Earth and not to the sky.

It seems that our record-keeping ancestors knew of relationships between earth, sky, and the spiritual realms that we have long forgotten. Careful reading of ancient mythology reveals that our ancestors had an awareness of the Great Year of the Precession of the Equinoxes.

The Great Year is the 26,000 year cycle during which the Earth's Northern axis point (by which the point of True North and the Pole Star are determined), when envisioned extending upward into space, describes the form of a great circle, or wheel, in the heavens. Determining North and orienting to the stars (for navigation reasons at the very least) has always been of the utmost importance. The stone "technology" developed to do so, and to maintain the knowledge down through the generations, was impressive and remains little understood to this day. The Sky Circle that formed over the 26,000 period certainly cannot have gone unnoticed or have been considered insignificant by our stargazing, spiritual-minded, but essentially pragmatic ancestors, especially since their mythologies have left us with stories of previous and future "Ages" or "Worlds," and stories of the movement from one of these to the next.

THE CENTER

The Center of the Circle has always been, spiritually and materially, a point of great significance. Our ancestors noted, symbolized, and depicted it in many ways. The still, unmoving center of the sky, around which the rest of the sky revolved (seen as the "Nail" in the sky's center by the Norse, the Chukchi of Eastern Siberia, and the Taoists of ancient China), had its counterpart on Earth. As above, so below. So we find references to World Trees and Mountains, Pyramids, Omphalos (navel or center) stones, Hitching Posts, Poles, Pillars, and Central Fires—all of them symbolizing the Center of the World, and by extension, the Universe.

The World Tree was seen as a huge tree, whose Underworld roots, trunk stretching skyward, and branches extending into the Upperworld, seemed to connect all these worlds, and serve as the way of passage between them. To the Norse this tree was Yggdrasil, the great ash tree; to the Mayans it was the ceiba or cottonwood tree. To the Omaha of the Nebraskan plains it was an evergreen cedar; in Siberia it was often a birch.

Some cultures saw the Center place as a "World Mountain," such as Mount Meru in the Vedic stories of India. It has been said that the ancient Egyptians considered the Great Pyramid to be located in the exact center of the world. Its shape suggests its relationship to the World Mountain.

The Sacred Circles we use ceremonially are ways of orienting ourselves to our world. As we sit inside the magical circles we have so carefully laid out, determining the compass points of East, South, West, and North, it becomes apparent that we who are inside the circle have become the center point. *We are, in fact, always the center of our own circle* because our physical beings have a front, back and sides, creating a personal equivalent to the Four Directions. So when we sit inside of our own circle, our magical circle of the self, we are the point at its center. We are the center point of a circle that exists, to all appearances, in a somewhat flat, horizontal reality.

But what if we take the vertical plane into account? This makes our flat, horizontal circle into a sphere, with a vertical axis running through it, above, through, and below us. The vertical axis, the Axis Mundi (World Axis), the Sacred Tree, the World Tree, the wizard's staff, the standing stones with their ends buried deep in the Earth—each of these are representative of the deep and important connection of below and above, Earth and sky, physical reality, and other realities. And in the center, the point of intersection of the Four Directions and the Above and Below, is the *Within*, the Sacred Self, we who have used this circle to orient ourselves to our world and our cosmos.

The important thing in all of the Center representations previously mentioned is that, in addition to being considered the point of Origin/Center of the World/Cosmos, they were seen to *connect* the Above and Below, Upperworlds with Lowerworlds. The World Mountain (Tree, Pillar, Pole, Hitching Post) was seen to be *the way between these worlds*, the path one took when traveling between them. This road made travel possible between the worlds. Therefore, one could approach the High Gods/Goddesses; one could travel to the Underworld home of the ancestral spirits and Underworld Gods/Goddesses by traversing this road. This is precisely what shamans, worldwide, are known to have done; they traveled the path that goes between the worlds.

So if we are always at the center of our *own* circle, then we, like the shamans, have the potential to travel between the worlds. But in this case, it is between the worlds of the self. From our everyday, mundane Middleworld, we can journey into the Lowerworlds of our ancestral bloodlines, and the places/states of being that lie deep within us. We may travel as well to the places of our own Upperworlds: places where our expanded, future, potential selves reside, and where we can connect with higher, transpersonal aspects of our selves.

The fact that tribal peoples have always seen themselves to be living at the center of the world or universe, and have referred to themselves as "the People" or "the Principal People," should alert us to the fact that they were aware of some great spiritual truths: the importance of the point of Center;

the knowledge that the center is wherever you are; and connection to our own heights and depths is essential to our wholeness.

It is the Center Point that is the point of Spirit. Thus it is our point of origin, the place from which our beingness originates and to which it returns. The sacred self within the Center of our own personal circle is the Spirit-Self Within. Our Spirit-Self-Within is our Total Self, the one not *exclusive* to this time, place, or incarnation; the one not suffering from, trapped in, or identified with our problems, situations, or addictions. Our Spirit-Self has a good perspective—360 degrees, as well as spherical vision—from its dwelling place in the Center perspective. It sees the total picture, not just this particular life, time, place, and situation in which we find our current body/mind/emotions/soul wrapped up. It sees *all* of our selves: past lives, future lives, parallel lives, other dimensions, and anything else there is to be seen.

This Spirit-Self, or Greater Self, is one whose very existence we sometimes lose sight of in our focus on our mental, emotional, or physical selves. It is important that we keep connected with this Spirit-Self, because to do so enables us to not only see a bigger, broader picture of how things are, but also allows us to get in touch with our deepest parts and issues, and approach them from a different angle. To be truly centered is to be conscious of, and in touch with, this part of ourselves.

It must be said here that most of us are confused or deceived about this part of our self. Our sense of self is frequently a result of our conditioning, experiences, addictions, and others' expectations of us, as well as our own self-judgment/condemnation about not living up to those expectations, or to our own expectations. As a result of this, we are often unconscious of our Spirit-Self, or confuse it with the particular behavioral or emotional patterns we are currently enacting. Its sort of like confusing the clothing with the person who is wearing it.

As we go through life, we find ourselves becoming polarized and/or caught in dualities.

This is true even when we are trying hard to use the polarities (see Chapter 9) to bring ourselves into balance. "Too much emotion," we might say to ourselves, "Time to use our minds a bit more." What can happen, in spite of our good intentions, is that we may find ourselves swinging wildly back and forth between the extremes of mind (Air) and emotion (Water), and never quite finding the place of balance where we are getting in touch with the Center. At this point, it is good to take a spiritual shortcut in order to get at the root of what is really going on that manifests in our wild extremes. It is our Spirit-Self, with its broader, deeper perspective, that can give us assistance here, by allowing us to see, to know, and to approach things from its unique perspective.

So how is it that we can actually discover our Spirit-Self? How can we even find it, lost as we sometimes feel in a morass of emotions, formed as we've all been by a seeming hodgepodge of experiences? How can we get back in touch with, and become conscious of, our Spirit-Self-Within, when we have finally realized our out-of-touch situation? Ah, that's the challenge of "Know Thyself."

One of the first tasks I was asked to undertake in my early magical training fell under the category of "Know Thyself." I was asked to do a self-evaluation. I was asked to watch myself, to really take a good look at myself. I was asked to make a private list, just for me, of what I considered to be my strong points and my weak points, and to categorize these elementally. So I did this, and have been doing it ever since. It's a lifetime kind of a job.

What's really going on when we do an exercise such as the self-evaluation I was asked to do, is that we are developing what I like to call the Watcher Within, the part of us that simply sees, watches, and observes our own words and actions. This Watcher Within does not judge or condemn, it merely observes, and reports to us what it has observed. To develop the Watcher Within is to develop *self-awareness*. Self-awareness is the first step toward learning to recognize our patterns, behaviors, reactions, addictions, and all the things that trigger them.

Since we can observe these "things" (i.e., patterns, behaviors, reactions, and addictions), it becomes quite clear that these things are not us, but are more like clothing we are currently wearing (or perhaps have been wearing for quite a while!). When we truly come to this realization, the next realization is that we have the power to *change* these patterns: the power of choice. We can choose to rethink things, to seek deeper understanding, to speak different words, to take different actions, to shift the energy.

But how to be sure that in so doing we are not merely "changing clothes"?

The surety comes from developing a strong sense of the feel of the Spirit-Self-Within, as well as the ability to recognize its voice. When we have developed this, it becomes our point of reference in evaluating the other energies we experience.

SACRED CIRCLE OF INNER POWERS

The importance of developing an awareness of the subtle qualitative differences—the "sound," and the "feel"—of our own inner energies is a spiritual imperative. We must train ourselves to distinguish the voice of Spirit-Self-Within from the many other inner voices we sometimes hear, and recognize its feel from other energies we feel. As with almost every other developmental task, the implementation of this one also can make use of the Sacred Circle and the Four Elements/Directions. The task of learning to recognize this voice requires that we work with our minds, emotions, soul, and bodies. All will give us cues, clues, and assistance. We must learn to recognize the sound of this voice, the feel of its energy quality, the emotion or lack of emotion we experience when hearing its voice, and any physical sensations we notice when it speaks to us. Prayer and meditation are used to good effect for this purpose. Opening inner dialogue with the Spirit-Self-Within, asking it to reveal itself, and listening carefully to what comes through, is also an excellent approach.

The following is *my* understanding of the process that occurs in developing and applying self-awareness. It involves *my* own particular view/vision of the inner pathways taken by energies that move through us (our psychic circuitry if you will), as we process the events and experiences life brings. I believe that as we experience life, the energy taken in follows certain pathways. Developing self-awareness allows us to see this process in action, noticing its parts. Self-awareness allows us to become conscious of this process, ultimately working *with* the process.

The energy movement pattern here is a version of the Lightningflash. The energy begins in the **East**; it moves through the **Center** to the **West**; along the edge of the Circle to the **Southwest**; then to the **South**; through **Center** again to the **North**; along the Circle edge to **Northeast**, continuing this movement till it finally comes back to the **East**. (See the illustration on page 121.)

This is how it works: The **Watcher Within** sees, informs, reports to us. This is the *East*, Air, the rather objective "power of the sword" which pierces through the veil of illusion. The **Listener Within** "hears" what was reported, takes it in, and reflects on (rather than judging or categorizing) what was heard. The Listener may even reflect back to the Watcher what was reported, just to be sure that the information was understood correctly. This is the *West*, the receiving and reflecting power of Water, the Cauldron which is able to contain all within.

Bear in mind that in order for this to happen, the "action" or energy must pass across the Center (see the diagram on page 121), thus allowing the perspective of the Spirit-Self-Within to subtly impact what is transiting across its "place." One might say this particular energy movement leaves a subtle imprint of the Spirit-Self.

As the energy transits from West to South, the **Senser Within** (not Censor!) of the *Southwest* "feels" what was reported, feels it out carefully, feels *into* it, noticing and filing away for future reference the subtle differences in energy qualities in all these things, *including the "imprint" of the Spirit-Self.*

By this point, things, impressions, states of being, and differing energetic qualities have been seen, reported, heard, and now "felt." The **Lightbearer Within** of the *South* is now called on to blaze forth, illuminating what has been taken in thus far, and allowing us to take a second and deeper, more thorough look, to *truly* see. The potential for growth to occur is now present, and the Lightbearer's assistance is required if we are to grow, as we now search for meaning in what's been observed/perceived/reflected upon. The Wand of disciplined Will now comes into play, providing the muscle, intention, skill, and precision that empower the next part of this Lightningflash energy movement.

The energy flashes across the Center again, and to the Knower or **Determiner Within** in the *North*, thus receiving another strong "*imprint*" from the Spirit-Self. The North is the place where our previous understanding/beliefs disintegrate as part of the natural process, falling away as new ways of understanding are opened by what has transpired within. Drawing upon the reports of the Watcher, the reflections of the Listener, the feeling/perceptions of the Senser, illuminated by the truthful blaze of the Lightbearer, our previous beliefs composted by the Determiner, we begin to discern the difference between the feel or voices of our conditioning/experiences/self-condemnation and that of our Spirit-Self, between the clothing and the one wearing the clothing. This is a *process*, and it takes time (some parts of it may take longer than others), though the ultimate realization sometimes comes through as a blinding flash of knowing (for me this part of the process is expressed as a palpable, almost physical, sensation). It rests within us for a while now.

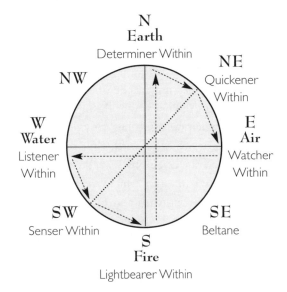

Sacred Circle of the Inner Powers

Then we find the energy passing across the *Northeast* Threshold of Quickening and Emergence on its way to birth at the *East.* The new understanding is born in the East; the Watcher Within registers the new ability, whose presence allows us to begin strategizing new options, based on what it has learned, and its clearer sense of identification with Spirit-Self.

The energy needs to flash across that Center point several times for the subtle "imprint" of the Spirit-Self to be registered sufficiently to be felt and differentiated from the rest of the impressions received. Once we begin to recognize the feel of the Spirit-Self (as distinct from the feel of the rest of the stuff), we can practice being in that feeling more often, feeling our way back into it when we find ourselves elsewhere (i.e., identifying ourself with an addiction or emotion). We can practice the art of "coming from that place" when we make our decisions, speak our words, and perform our actions. By practicing this, we become more proficient; we gain skill. We finally get beyond the place where we identify ourselves with our patterns, and recognize we have the power of choice in our responses.

This is only one way of approaching the issue of getting in touch with the Spirit-Self-Within, and it may or may not be the one that is appropriate for you. Another way is through ceremony. Sometimes when we are feeling very disconnected with our Spirit-Self, it is worthwhile to take time for a small private ceremony wherein we envision our smaller self (the self which we are currently incarnating) meeting with and merging with our Spirit-Self. This can be a very simple ceremony; the important part is to see but especially *feel* it as clearly as possible.

If we are to recapture the wisdom of our ancestors and recreate it for ourselves and our children in this day and age, if we are to build ourselves new ways of relating to life that are both wholistic and healing of the damage that has been done through the last two millennia, we need to remember to look up as well as down and look also, most especially, within—to the Sacred Self, the Spirit-Self—that is the connecting point of all these dimensions, the Center of the Circle.

We are multidimensional beings (to use New Age parlance), and it is of great importance for the future that we learn to navigate in a multidimensional way. Many of us are so busy looking where to place our feet as we plod forward—one foot in front of the other, getting through our daily grind—that we forget to look up. Others of us are so busy thinking or fantasizing about other realms of existence (or about the future) that we forget to look down to find secure footing. Either of these ways can lead to a lack of balance, causing us to stumble and fall. Both of these ways alone fail to anchor us in the Center Point of "within." Whether by looking upwards we fail to notice the abyss we are approaching and thus fall into it, or by looking downward we do not see the approaching rainclouds and thus find ourselves surprisingly cold and wet, we are missing at least half of our possible experiences, and possibilities of balance.

CENTER POINT CORRESPONDENCES

With regard to Element/Chakra correspondence, the Center Point corresponds to all the Elements, but none in particular. You will have noticed that in the preceding chapters, the sixth and seventh chakras were not discussed in relation to a particular Element. Traditionally, these two chakras are assigned to the province of the spiritual realms: Aether, Space, or Spirit, as it is variously called.

According to TCM, there is a river of energy in the human body (at the etheric body level) that runs from the coccyx (tailbone) up the spine, over the skull, and down the front midline of the body. This path of energy interacts with, regulates, and equalizes the other flows of energy throughout the body. This pathway is called the Great Central Channel. On its path from the coccyx, up the spine, over the skull to a point just below the nose, it is referred to as the Governing Vessel. Down the midline of the body from the point just below the mouth, it is referred to as the Conception Vessel. "Conception" refers, of course, to the reproductive faculties which this vessel influences in addition to influences on the lower abdomen in general. It is said that this vessel influences the state of spiritual peace or lack of peace. The Governing Vessel influences the spine and regulates prenatal (or inherited, often called ancestral) energy. It also influences the state of nervous stability or instability.

Since this river of energy lines up exactly with the spinal column, it runs through and connects all our chakras, root to crown, and therefore connects all the Elements. So the energy path of the spinal cord, the vertical Center of our bodies, *becomes our own World Tree,* our own Pole or Pillar, with energy spiraling upward and downward. In this particular flow, the energy from our earthy root chakra near the perineal region is connected with the energy of our heavenly crown region on the top of the head. Within the brain are *dendrites,* branch-like structures that connect nerve endings and carry nerve signals throughout the brain (from the Greek *drys*, which means tree, and *dendro*, tree-like). These are our "branches," and "branchlets," connecting us to the Upperworld, just as our root chakra and the roots of our legs/feet connect us to the Lowerworld. So like the great World Tree, we are rooted in the Earth, yet connected to the sky by our "crown" of branches, dendrites (which, by the way, increase in number as we use our mind/intellect). As use of these mind/intellect faculties is intimately related to our physical experience of life, we can see how it is that the root feeds the crown, and yet the crown also feeds the root, in an endless spiraling of energies from above and below.

The site of the sixth chakra, the pineal gland, lies within the center of the brain. The tiny, light-sensitive pineal is related to the body's circadian rhythms (day/night, light/dark, waking/sleeping) and possibly to reproduction, but has traditionally been associated with the psychic vision of the "third eye." The Chinese philosopher Lao Tzu called the pineal the "gateway between heaven and earth." It has also been known in the East as the "cavity of spirit." Perhaps the pineal is the fruit of enlightenment on the branches of our tree, or perhaps it represents the bird frequently depicted as sitting within the branches of the World Tree (in shamanic world views), who is symbolic of spiritual consciousness.

In some systems of chakra correspondences, it is the pituitary gland rather than the pineal that is associated with the sixth chakra; the pineal is then said to be associated with the seventh chakra. The pituitary gland, which is said to exhibit phosphorescence, is considered the master gland of the body's endocrine system, due to the fact that it secretes hormones affecting reproduction, physical growth, stress reaction, blood pressure, and many

other things. Since both of these glands have wide-ranging functions, they seem to correspond to the very tips of the wide crown of branches of our tree.

What I have just described represents the vertical version of the Center Point. But let us not forget the horizontal aspect: the Center as the place where all directional/elemental paths meet, and yet the seed from which they spring; the place which I have previously described as the Cauldron simmering and steaming over the Hearthfire of Life (see Chapter 2). This "center" is our physical center as viewed from the horizontal plane. Together, these two—the vertical (which seems masculine) and the horizontal (which seems feminine)—seem to be illustrating for us the two-in-one, the God/Goddess, the Yin/Yang, that is our true Center, point of origin and return.

Interestingly, in TCM the Governing Vessel is seen as masculine or yang in nature, while the Conception Vessel is seen as feminine or yin in nature. In India, this relationship of energies is conceptualized as two serpents, the masculine, solar *Pingala*, and the feminine, lunar *Ida*, twining their way up and down the spinal column, or *Sushumna*.

There is an obvious similarity here to the figure of the caduceus (adopted by our modern medical profession as the sign of the healer), which originated in ancient Egypt as the staff of Tehuti or Thoth, but is also found in Greece and Central America. The caduceus as a symbol of the healing arts shows us, whether our modern healers remember it or not, that true healing involves balanced energies and a relationship to the Center.

CENTERING PRACTICES

The following meditations and exercises are useful for working with the Center Point.

CENTER MEDITATION

You find that you are standing in the central firepit of a Great Circle. The fire is burning. Looking down at yourself, you see that your body is glowing, merged with the flame. As you observe yourself, it seems to you that your body has become a great, glowing tree, standing, branches outspread, in the Center of this Circle. From your Center vantage point, you turn slowly and notice that each of the Directions is marked by a gateway of two standing stones. You pause briefly as you face each of the Directions, looking through the gateway, taking note of what you see on the other side of it. (PAUSE) You are aware, as you face each of the Directions in turn, of the energy of that particular Direction, and its corresponding Element, flowing through the gateway and to the Center of the Circle. You tune into this experience for a few moments (PAUSE), and it is then that you notice that the energy, in reality, goes both directions. You feel it as it flows into the Circle and toward the Center, through the gateways. You now also feel it as it wells up from the Center and flows outward in the direction of the four gateways. Spend some time noticing and feeling this. (PAUSE)

Now you place your full attention on the Center place where you are standing. As you do this you feel lengthened, and notice that the energy seems to flow upward from beneath you, through you, and skyward. This phenomena seems to induce a feeling of length, of height; you feel yourself extending deep into the ground and high up into the sky. You are aware that the tree that is you has roots which grow deep into the ground, and branches that extend high and wide, upward. Spend a few moments feeling this, noting the subtle qualities of each of these things. (PAUSE)

Though you feel yourself to be tree-like, you find you can move. Feel yourself extending your arms/branches outward from your sides and slowly turning in a clockwise direction. Feel how your being, which now extends deep into the earth and high into the sky, scoops up the energies and qualities of each Direction/Element as you revolve past each Direction. Visualize yourself turning, revolving, scooping energy from each Direction, for nine turns, then come to a stop. Notice how you feel. (PAUSE) Gather the energy you have scooped up into the shape of a large ball, then offer it to Earth or sky, whichever feels appropriate to you. (PAUSE) Bring your arms/branches back down to your sides. Breathe deeply and exhale, slowly bringing yourself back to the present time and place. When you feel ready, open your eyes.

SHOWERING OF STARS: THE EARTHSTAR MEDITATION

This exercise was given to me in meditation a few years back, and has proved to be a powerful addition to my spiritual repertoire. In some ways it is a more advanced version of the tree exercise above. This exercise is best done standing.

Take a deep breath. Feel yourself to be growing roots from the soles of your feet and from your root chakra (allow your attention to be with these roots during the entire rooting process). Exhale, and allow this exhalation to carry your roots deep down into the Earth. As you begin to descend, be aware of the creatures of Earth: plants, animals, insects, Nature Spirits—and greet them. As you continue to descend, be aware of the Faery realms, the Ancestral realms, and any other Underworld realms and planetary Beings you may encounter. Give your greetings to these Beings also. Extend your roots ever downward, till you have come to the Fireheart of the earth, and the iron crystal core within it. Anchor your roots here.

Allow the energy from Earth's Heart to ascend upward through your roots, again, greeting any Beings you may encounter along the way. Bring this energy upward and into your body, first through your roots and into the feet, then legs, torso, chest, arms, hands, neck, and head. Feel yourself filled with this energy.

Feel the energy running through your chakras. Place your attention on this for a few moments, and feel the energy spiraling up your chakras from root to crown. Feel the energy moving out of you at the crown chakra and spiraling upward into the sky and beyond. Feel it, follow it, as it spirals upward, encountering and passing through the Moon. Spend a few moments communing with the Moon, giving your greetings and love. Notice how you feel when communing with the Moon. Feel the energy continue spiraling

outward, encountering and passing through the Sun. Give greetings and love to the Sun. Spend a moment feeling this communion.

Passing through the Sun, you feel the energy continuing now into the depths of space. Greet the Stars as you come to them, traveling with the spiraling energy as it moves along the spiraling arm of our home galaxy, the Milky Way, and to the very center of the galaxy. Feel the burst of energy as you connect with, and go into, this great Source. Spend some time being with this, feeling, noticing, communing.

Feel the energy flow downward towards you, spiraling now in the opposite direction on the arms of the galaxy. Feel it flow downward, through the Sun, the Moon, toward the Earth, downward and into your body, passing through your body and into the Earth. As it passes through your body, notice how it combines with the Earth energy therein.

Be aware that the energy spirals both upward and downward at the same time. Feel the Sky-Earth energy exchange happening through you as you simultaneously "feed" Earth-to-Sky and Sky-to-Earth. You are a conduit, therefore this energy runs through you, leaving its plenteous residue to feed you also. You are a Child of Earth and Sky.

Spread your arms, hold them out from your body and parallel the ground so that your body forms a Star, and shower Sky Energy into the Earth. Lift your arms to the Sky and radiate Earth Energy to the Sky.

You, as human, act as a bridge between the Earth and Star energies, since by your heritage you partake of both. When you are finished, bring your arms back down to your sides. Breathe in and out slowly and deeply, and bring your consciousness back to its normal state.

CENTER EXERCISES

1. Consult some reference books, and see what you can find out about World Trees, World Mountains, Omphalos stones, Central Fires, hitching posts, pillars, Sundance Trees, and tent poles as symbols of the Center Point of Earth, Sky, or Cosmos.

2. Become a tree. Feel yourself growing roots from your root chakra and from the soles of your feet. Feel your body becoming the trunk, and feel your arms and upper body turning into branches and leaves. Feel your branches reaching out into the cosmos, and down into the Earth. Bring energy up from where your roots entwine with the heart of the Earth. Bring energy down from where your branches touch the heart of the Cosmos. Feel the energy as it runs upward and downward along your trunk. Feel the energy as it runs out along your branches and into your twigs and leaves. After a while, bring your awareness back to your current physical self, time, and place.

3. Similarly, become a mound, a mountain, or pyramid. Notice how there is a corresponding energy field of the same shape beneath you, so that in a sense your shape approaches that of a diamond. In this way you, as a mound, mountain, or pyramid, experience the Underworld and Overworld at the same time. Your essence is the fire in the center of the diamond. Feel all of this as you point upward to the galactic center/fireheart, as well as down to the Earth's core/fireheart. Now feel your sides and edges. Feel to your right, your left, before you, behind you. Notice how, or if, these are oriented to the directional points of ESWN. Feel your essence, your Self, centered within all of this.

4. Many cultures have had Sacred Circle Dances which involved spinning. Using the Center visualization on page 124 as a starting point, create your own circle dance. Through your dance, create the world. Feel yourself as Center, with energy flowing forth from you to become the power of the Elements and Directions. Begin spinning to your right, scooping up the Elemental energies as you do so, and allow the creative power of the Great Mystery to flow through you and outward. Stop when all feels complete to you.

5. Practice the self-awareness technique described in the section "Sacred Circle of the Inner Powers" on pages 120-122. Keep a journal of your experiences and thoughts while doing this.

6. Every night before going to sleep, recount your day to yourself, starting with the most recent things and working back towards morning. This technique helps memory, and lets you take a second look at not only the things that occurred, but also your reaction to them. It gives you an opportunity to reflect on the choices you have made during the course of your day, and think about whether you'd make the same choice again if a similar situation arose.

CHAPTER NINE

Balancing the Elements—
the Sacred Human

Take a deep breath,
Keep your Hearthfire burning,
Flow with your emotions,
Ground into your life.

Humans are composed of all of the Elements, in various measures. All of the Elements are important to human life and survival; deprived of any one of them, our lives would end.

Looked at another way, Air is the *Breath of Life*, Fire is the *Spark of Life*, Water is the *Flow of Life*, Earth is the *Structure of Life*, and Spirit, which permeates them all and weaves them all together, is the *Seed and Source, Origin and End Point*. Spirit permeates all the Elements and weaves them together.

We humans are born from the Spirit world into the Physical world. We are created of the Spirit-filled Elements and bring our spark of Spirit essence into this life with us. To mediate our consciousness between the two extremes of Unmanifest Spirit and Manifest Spirit is the job of our soul.

It is our job as humans to keep ourselves healthy, by tending to and keeping in proper balance the Elements of Life as they occur on both inner and outer levels. What this practically translates into, and ideas on striving for balance, are the subjects of this chapter.

There are many metaphors one can use to name and describe this process, but here are the two that I find most useful: Keeping the Hearth,

and Balancing the Shields (a Native American term used for the personal version of working with the Elemental/Directional powers). These two ways of looking at the process really work well together. If we work at keeping our shields balanced, we are automatically tending our hearthfire. If we tend our hearthfire, we are automatically balancing our shields.

The Hearthfire is the Life Fire: our personal spark of Mother Life (or Life Force). To live it, to experience it, to be conscious within it, to honor it, and to caretake it are sacred tasks; these are our responsibilities as Sacred Humans. To caretake it, in ourselves and others, is to keep it alive—*to keep life happening,* to aid Mother Life's process. We are not separate from this, but a part of it.

To keep the Fires of our Hearth healthy, to keep them burning brightly and clearly, is to work with the Elements of our life to assure that all are there in proper amount and balance.

What are the Elements of our life? Well, refer again to that wonderful glyph of the Sacred Circle, and you will see. As we consider each of the Directions and Elements this time, we are going to travel the path of the Lightningflash—the active path of creative movement—in moving through the positions of the Wheel.

All the aspects are, of course, interwoven, and one could begin working this Wheel from almost any place. The best way I've found is to study each of the Directions, to reflect on what you are learning, and as you do so, your own imbalances will become clearer to you. Pick one that seems to call out loudest to you, decide with which Element/Direction it seems most connected, and begin working on it.

Remember this, however, our subtle bodies are just as real as our physical bodies. The problems and challenges we face might have their origin in one or more of our subtle bodies. *All* of our bodies (subtle and physical) need to take in nourishment and to eliminate waste. They need exercise. We form them from what we take into them and how it is processed: digested, assimilated, eliminated. If you feed your physical body good food, but nourish your mental, emotional, and spiritual bodies on junk food, guess what's going to happen to the health of those bodies, and to your total health and well being?

EAST—PLACE OF THE MIND

Let's begin in the East, the place of our minds, the mental aspect of ourselves. Our minds are the source of our thoughts. And you've heard it before but I'll say it again: *thoughts are things.* Our power to create begins with a thought (which sometimes comes to us in the form of an "inspiration"). What we do with our thoughts, which ones we choose to hang out with (keep in our minds) and which ones we choose to discard, is quite relevant to our state of balance or imbalance.

All of us have many, many thoughts traveling through our minds in the course of a minute, an hour, a day, a week, a month. Some are very transient (*I'd better not forget to put the trash out*). Some are part of our thought patterns (*I'll never really be happy in my job*). Thoughts and emotions both originate in the mind and are very tied together. Emotions are, in a sense, our experience of energy movement in response to thought. Emotions are our "feeling awareness" of the energy we give to thoughts, and the way in which we give it. Sometimes we spend so much energy on a thought that it becomes a "thought form," a

much more powerful entity than a mere, brief, passing thought. The thought form exerts a power of its own and has a tendency to want to keep itself in existence.

All day long we are barraged with images and events that seem to demand that we think about them. It is important that we learn to choose what thoughts we will hang out with—that we will feed energy into—and those we will not. Choice is the important word here. This does not mean that we will ignore or deny unpleasant things and hope they will go away. It means we will choose *how* we think of them so as to reap the best possible learning from them and not get stuck in a downward swirling vortex of scattered or negative thinking that will create a thought-form that we'd rather not meet in a dark alley at night.

What we are being called on to do here is to tend to the proper nourishment of our Mental Body, to its correct education, to the cultivation of good thought and nourishing patterns of thinking, to the elimination of ideas and thoughts whose service to us has been completed.

The challenge is to set our ideals as to what we would like to manifest in our lives and choose thoughts that support those ideals. In a way, it is like gardening. Choose what you would plant, create the proper conditions for it, plant it, keep it weeded and watered and, if weather conditions offer support, you will reap a good harvest. Given the choice, most of us would like to cultivate serenity and prosperity in the garden of our lives. This necessitates that we make choices to turn aside the possible formation of thought-patterns of fear, anger, and doubt. When situations come up, as they inevitably will, that engender such thoughts and emotions, it is wise for us to experience these as they flow through us (and keep them flowing), but to choose not only how we will *respond,* but also how we will *interpret* the situation in the light of our path of learning and the garden we are cultivating. To do this is to cultivate (and feed energy into) thought-forms that are beneficial to us and to our lives. Our mental bodies themselves can be seen as thought-forms that we create by the choices we make with regard to our thinking/feeling about life and ourselves.

WEST—PLACE OF EMOTIONS

All of this is so very tied into emotions that the next part of the Wheel we need to move to is the West, the place of our emotions. The dictionary tells us that "Emotion" is from the French *emouvoir*, meaning "to stir up," and the Latin *ex movere*, meaning "to move away." By this definition, our emotions are our awareness of the agitation, the stirring up, the movement of thought-engendered energy as it flows through us: Energy in motion. Emotions have been likened to thoughts with feeling attached to them. Our thoughts *engender* emotions and our emotions *empower* (and sometimes give rise to further) thoughts. We say we feel *happy, excited, fearful, sad,* or *angry;* and just saying it, realizing it, identifying it, demonstrates our awareness of the these feeling-energy rivers that stream through us.

There's more to it than that, however. Emotions can be subtle sometimes, so to name and identify them frequently only gets at the big ones (and naming/identifying is a mental function, showing again the way Air/Water, Thought/Emotion are tied together). At any given moment we are experiencing a vast array of subtle feelings about a vast array of occurrences or thoughts. Take a moment and tune into what you are feeling now, at this moment. If you are like me there are several things going on. Part of me is feeling quite contented because I just finished a wonderful, healthful dinner. Part of me is feeling mildly annoyed because the radio is up too loud in the kids' room next door to me. I am aware that I've been sitting here writing for too many hours today and should go take a walk (the walk to and from the dinner table doesn't count). But I don't want to take a walk, and there's a part of me that feels guilty because of that. Part of me

is a bit worried because earlier today I heard something ecologically worrisome on the news.

Now most of these feelings are transient: they will keep on flowing right through me; some of this stuff will sort itself out, some of it I'll forget about. I could choose to tell the kids to turn the radio down. Maybe the kids will decide to turn it off and solve the problem. Or maybe I will make a choice to listen to and appreciate the music and then it won't seem too loud anymore. Maybe I'll deal with the guilt about not taking a walk by choosing to rationalize my way out of it (*my writing is more important than a walk right now; I'll take one tomorrow*); or maybe I'll decide to interpret the guilt feeling as a message from my body that it really needs some exercise and make a choice to go out for a walk. (*Hmm, sounds good. I'll be back in about 1/2 an hour!*) But what can I do about the worry I'm feeling due to the worrisome news I heard earlier on a radio broadcast? I cannot personally affect *this* cause of what I am feeling, I cannot make it go away. But I *can* choose to send some healing energy in the direction from which it came, and turn my focus elsewhere. I can *choose* not to follow the path of worry till it turns into fear—a fear of maybes, a fear of "what-ifs," a fear of "I don't know where this will lead and there's nothing I can do about it"—and then from fear into being overwhelmed.

As you can see, the point I am trying to illustrate is choice—choice with emotions as well as with thoughts. Do we choose to *react* to situations or to *respond*? Choice does not deny the reality of the feeling, it decides what to do about the feeling—sometimes, in the process, figuring out what is creating the feeling. Ideally, it chooses to allow the feeling the full range of motion it needs to keep flowing.

To be healthy, emotions need to stay "in motion." It is easy to see how emotions are related to the Water Element, which also needs to stay in motion lest it become stagnant. When emotions do not flow they get stuck, stagnant, and stale, and usually build up inside of us, affecting health of both mind and body. Sometimes the lack of flow can lead to a dangerous build-up that results, when finally released, in an emotional flood of dangerous proportions.

In the West, we are being called to the proper tending of our Emotional bodies, which means allowing them to express themselves fully and properly, so that what needs to flow through does not get stuck within us and cause unnecessary damage to ourselves and others. Remember, the West is the place of nourishment and harvest. A diet of junk food for the Emotional body (negative or stuck emotions) will result in its ill health, a bad harvest indeed. Do we really want to "form" our Emotional bodies out of the energies of *constant* sorrow, grief, anger, or fear? It is important, when we are experiencing situations that bring up these emotions, to also remember the lesson of water, and let things keep flowing. Express your emotions by doing things that keep the energy moving and flowing, such as playing music, making art, dancing/moving, talking, screaming, writing, drumming, or performing ceremony. Once, when I was living through a time of great grief, I found that the only thing that helped me move through it was listening again and again and again to a certain very dramatic piece of music. I did this for months; I found my grief draining away. Experience the emotion, really be in it, get all the feeling and learning you can from it. Let it—like the ocean—experience its high and low tides; but always keep a sense of flow, and eventually, let the tide take it out and away.

Realize here that I am not referring to a state of clinical depression. This is a serious problem of imbalance in which emotions are not flowing properly, are backlogged and stuck, sometimes for very physical reasons of chemical imbalance. This problem needs to be dealt with in physical ways, by correcting the chemical imbalance (first stop the hemorrhage, then tend the wounds). The other methods then become appropriate to maintain the balance and heal the emotional patterns that created the physical imbalance. Acupuncturists have many good alternative treatments for depression.

The West reminds us to be aware of the rhythm of tides. Things flow in, and they flow out. High tide, with all its drama and crashing waves, may seem like it's going to last forever, but it won't. The low tide will come in its turn, and things will change.

This having been said, I must also say that there are times in dealing with emotion when choice comes into play in a different way: emotional catharsis. All of us occasionally go through cathartic situations in life. There are certain schools of thought that dictate that no real healing has occurred if one has not gone through major cathartic release of emotions, maybe several times.

My feeling is that this can be dangerous territory. Emotions are not only like flowing rivers and tumultuous oceans, they can also be like endlessly deep wells. Sometimes, in states of extreme emotion, it seems like what we are feeling will never end. It goes on and on and on. We may plumb the depths, and they seem endless. I have experienced this personally, and felt after a while that I had fallen into, and was tumbling deeper and deeper into, the well of collective emotion, and feeling it as my own. It was difficult to tell the difference. How long can one weep, grieve, or fear without tapping into *all* the sorrow, pain, and fear in the world? Endless emoting can be *extremely* depleting physically and energetically. There comes a time when we must somehow return to normal functioning. The choice here then becomes a decision to heal; to stop swimming around in our intense, seemingly endless feelings, and move on, get on with our lives.

Emotions and thought-forms may be more powerful than we realize. Every day brings more news of how scientists are discovering a genetic basis for everything from behaviors to disease susceptibility. If looked at from a strictly "materialist" world view, this would seem to suggest that we are simply a result of our genes—from our diseases, to our emotions, to our behaviors. And if this is so, then there isn't much to be done about all these things, aside from resorting to some sort of physical, genetic alteration to the parts of ourselves that we find faulty.

I began thinking about this genetic issue in relation to my own birth family, pondering the hereditary physical and mental tendencies I see being passed down through the generations. I wondered about the nature of the mechanism that causes certain genes to mutate and become abnormal. I wondered if such a mechanism was hereditary, and if so, what caused the hereditary mechanism to evolve into being in the first place. Instantly my mind booted up for my consideration a menu of the emotional patterns I've seen carried from generation to generation within my family. With a start, I realized that emotion, mind, and soul played a great part in these problems, greater than I had previously realized. I had looked at both the physical and subtle components before, but never simultaneously. When I considered them together, they fit together in a seamless way.

Emotion is "energy in motion." If this energy-in-motion is capable of acting upon DNA on a very subtle level, (i.e., that level of matter/energy interface which physicists are currently examining), this emotional energy could quite possibly generate change in the cellular structure at the DNA level. This change might then, quite conceivably, be passed down through the generations. It follows that if we (and our scientific researchers) look only at the physical, genetic structure of disease, we will see its "cure" only by physically, manipulative means. But this fails to address the question of why the gene mutated to abnormality in the first place, and the further question of what would keep the same mutational process from occurring again in the future. A human being is an intricate, complex weaving of energies and relationships. It seems to me that the true answers to such complex questions are to be found only if we look at emotional, mental, and spiritual levels of disease, as well as the physical.

SOUTH—PLACE OF SOUL AND SPIRIT

An important and frequently overlooked aspect of ourselves, one which directly affects how we handle our thoughts and feelings, is the part of us related to the South: the place of Soul and Spirit. Spirit permeates all the Elements and Directions, but this particular Direction, connected as it is with Fire, via the Soul, is a major portal for direct recognition of the principle of Spirit in a very personal sense. (See Chapter 4.)

The fiery, South aspect of ourselves is on a constant quest for truth, light, meaning, and healing. As such, it serves to "ignite" the other aspects of us and motivate them to keep going. Yet this fire definitely needs to be fed. How do we feed it? By "tending" to our spiritual life.

The South is also the place of Will, and often we need to exercise this "will muscle," the power of our intention, to persist in our efforts to tend our spiritual lives.

It is important to take time for our spiritual practices. Whatever meditations, prayers, and rituals we deem to be our spiritual practices are just as important as the food we eat, the air we breathe, and the water we drink. We are not properly nourished without tending this aspect of ourselves.

We need time alone, and time with others. We need our self-crafted, personal rituals, as well as ones we do with others. These personal ceremonies honor what we are experiencing and mark it with a validating awareness. This is Soul Food of the highest order! We need spiritual times with others, though this need not always be a time when we are doing "spiritual things" or having "spiritual talks." We need times when our spirits connect with one another in a deep way that can be passionate, expressive, creative, and fun. Our sexual fires fall under this governance of South also, since they are the fires of our creativity, though not all "fiery," passionate encounters are necessarily physically sexual.

In fact, tending our sexual fires is extremely important since they are, indeed, the fires of our creativity. There is a close relationship between sexuality and spirituality. The Creative Fire that brought the universe into being was the ultimate sexual fire, since fusion of two polarities is the source of creativity on all levels of being. Properly tended sexual fires (creativity) lead to healthy conception and birth of new life on all levels of being.

Whatever we create in life, whether it be a baby or a business, goes through the same process: It is *conceived*, it is *gestated* (and must be properly cared for during the gestation process), and at length there is "*labor*"—a process of hard work by which it is finally *born*—brought forth into the world of manifestation. After it is born it needs additional care, nurturing, and attention till it grows self-sufficient enough to take off on its own.

NORTH—PLACE OF PHYSICAL MANIFESTATION

And what is it to birth something? It is to manifest it, to give it form. This brings us around to the North, the place of physical manifestation and of our physical selves.

All infants need care, being too young to fend for themselves. When we were babies our parents or other adults cared for us, making sure we received proper nourishment and love, without which we would have failed to thrive.

But now we are adults, and the care of our physical selves is our job to take on.

Our relationship with physicality in general needs to be kept healthy. Not only do we need to take proper care of these wonderful physical bodies of ours, but we need to maintain a healthy relationship to them and to the rest of the physical, material world. What is our relationship to and our feelings about the trees, the flowers, the stones, other people, Mother Earth? To our possessions, our money, our talents, and abilities?

We all know we need to brush our teeth, keep our bodies clean, eat nourishing food, and get enough exercise. But to really take care of our earthy, physical selves, we must also take care of the other three aspects of ourselves—our "airy" minds, our "watery" emotions and souls, and our "fiery" souls/spirits—because all of them together make up who we are. We are not just physical bodies, the body is the grounding point for the other three. Without it, we are without a "form" of Self-Expression on this plane of existence (which is obviously where we have *chosen* to be or we wouldn't be here!).

Here are some suggestions for Keeping Your Hearth/Balancing Your Shields:

NOURISH AND CARE FOR YOUR MENTAL, EMOTIONAL, AND SPIRITUAL BODIES.

Live in tune with the seasons.
The cultural disease of "separation mentality" dictates to us that we are not really a part of it all, but separate, outside, watching it happen (and can therefore, manipulate it around to our own preference). This, of course, is not true. We are more affected by the physical seasons of Mother Earth than we care to admit to ourselves, accustomed as we are to artificial lighting and forced air heating. Try living through an earthquake, blizzard, cyclone, or hurricane if you think you are separate from the rest of Nature. In a very real way, we are Earth, and we have our seasons too, a fact we ignore at our own peril.

Living in tune with Earth's seasons helps us to live in tune with our own. Developing correct eating and sleeping patterns as part of our spiritual/physical practices will go a long way toward such alignment. Learning about our physical bodies, their needs and desires, and how they function is also important.

Living with the seasons means choosing what you eat, wear, and do, bearing in mind whether it is Spring, Summer, Winter, or Fall. During Winter it is cold, the days are short. Your body needs to be kept warm so that your vital organs can do their job properly. You may feel a need to hibernate, to sleep and dream more during Winter than during other times of the year. Honor this by choosing warmer foods—soups, stews, hearty things—and by staying home a lot, and allowing yourself time to be internal. Summer is the opposite. You'll more likely be wanting to enjoy the longer days, partying with friends, keeping cool with lots of salads and fruits. Honor this too. Enjoy whatever season is occurring, really get into it. Don't pretend that all days are the same, that all seasons are the same.

Develop a true respect for all the Elements of Life.

Respect Earth as substance and sensuality. Respect Air as breath, electricity, movement, and the rhythms of expansion/contraction in the forms of inhalation/exhalation and nourishment/elimination. Respect Water as "motion and emotion," ebb and flow, high tides, and low, and by extension, all life's rhythms. Respect Fire as will (our power of intention) and soul: the personal indwelling vehicle of spirit, that personal spark of divine life that makes our own life possible.

You've got to keep all the Elements in balance if you want to keep your Hearthfire burning. Excessive Earth will smother it; excessive Air can whip it into an uncontrollable destructive frenzy; excessive Water will drown it for sure (as well as rendering your firewood unusable and leaving your hearth a place of soggy ash!).

We can use our physical body as a metaphor for the process of working on attaining balance in our lives. Proper nourishment must be provided. We "consume" experiences and then must "digest" them. The digestive process decides which of these experiences, and our feelings about them, can be assimilated and used, and which need to be eliminated. But the digestive fires must be in good working order for this to occur. If we have honored their needs they will serve us well. If we have honored the needs of our inspiration/expiration system for a clean atmosphere, it will serve us well by separating out the thoughts and feelings that serve no purpose of nourishment and allowing them to be exhaled. It will deposit the nutritious nuggets of experience, inspiration, and feelings into our bloodstreams. If we have honored the needs of our heart to love and be loved, it will keep this rich, clean, blood flowing through our bodies to nourish every cell.

The first law of Nature is Self-Preservation: Life is designed to continue, to carry on, to sustain itself. Learn to cooperate with this process, instead of trying to force yourself into unnatural channels.

THE WHEEL OF BALANCE

Here's something else to think about. Take a look at the wheels below and notice how the energies flow. In the Craft we talk a lot about opposites being "complementary" rather than "conflicting" opposites. This means that their functions and qualities are complementary to each other: They enhance, balance, and empower one another, rather than being conflicting or discordant. Looking at the Wheel, you will notice that Air is across from (opposite) Water, and that Fire and Earth are across from each other. Air = *Mind,* and Water = *Emotions*; Fire = *Soul/Spirit,* and Earth = *Body.* What this is really telling us is that Mind and Emotions are complementary to each others, and that Body and Spirit are complementary to each other.

What this means is that Fire and Earth (*Soul/Spirit* and *Body*) balance each other by sitting across from each other on the Wheel. Water and Air (*Emotions* and *Mind*) balance each other by sitting across from each other on the Wheel. What's on one side can serve as antidote for an excess or deficiency on the other side.

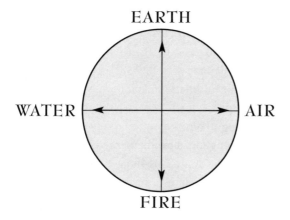

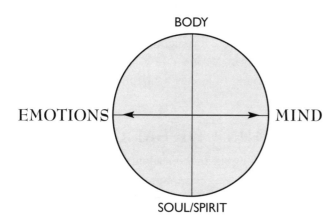

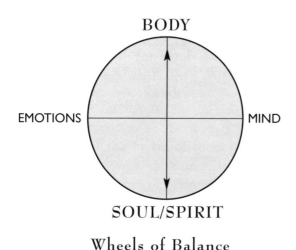

Wheels of Balance

Too much *Emotion* can be brought to balance by cultivating clear *Mind*. The medium (modus operandi) for this is Spirit/Soul; listen to what those emotions are telling you, and ask your inner Spirit-Self to let you know what it means.

Too much *Mind* can be brought to balance by allowing *Emotions* to flow. The medium for this is to pay attention to what the body is saying. We are all aware that our body gives us messages, some none too subtle. Yet we are all guilty of chalking up that sudden sensation or that pain seemingly from nowhere to chance, suppressing the accompanying emotion as it tries to arise, and allowing the mind to continue its ceaseless chatter, rationalizing something that perhaps ought not be rationalized.

Too much *Body* can be brought to balance by bringing *Spiritual* practices to bear. The medium for this is the flow of Emotions. Allow yourself to really feel your emotions and you may notice a spiritual homesickness. An excessive focus on the physical realm can cause awareness of the spiritual realms to be clouded, overwhelmed by the day-to-day details.

Too much *Soul/Spirit* can be brought to balance by grounding more into the *Body's* needs (and the physical plane in general), and the medium for this is the discerning mind. Sometimes the piercing power of the Sword of Air is needed to separate true need from desire, lest we lose ourselves in a blissful, constant attention to spiritual rather than physical matters.

We must, by how we live, demonstrate respect for all the Elements of Life: Earth *(substance, sensuality, malleability)*, Air *(electricity, movement, breath of life, rhythm of expansion/contraction, nourishment-elimination)*, Water *(motion, emotion, and life's rhythms)* and Fire *(soul, personal vehicle for indwelling spirit-spark of divine life making our own possible)*. Since these Elements of Life are the elements of our own lives and selves, by respecting them, we respect ourselves, as well as the Greater Life/Self.

I can see how a question might arise at this point. Though the other three might be easy to figure out, what would an imbalance or excess of Soul/Spirit be? What would it look like? A Soul/Spirit imbalance is made manifest in one of two ways: a disregard for, or aversion to, the physical body or the physical plane in general, or a desire to pursue only the spiritual, nonphysical aspect of life. If you find that you have a real, ongoing tendency to disregard your body's *needs* (as opposed to its continual *desires*), considering them unimportant, unworthy of your attention, or something to be denied or "affirmationed" away— you have imbalanced Fire/Earth Shields. If you find you have a tendency to immerse yourself exclusively in so-called spiritual thoughts, practices, or pursuits (in preference to eating, sleeping, cleaning your house, holding down a job, or maintaining a relationship), you have imbalanced Fire/Earth Shields. As mentioned above, the remedy for balancing these is to focus on the sacred and spiritual aspects of eating, sleeping, housecleaning, having a job, and maintaining a relationship. All of these tasks give honor to Spirit manifesting physically.

REAWAKENING THE SACRED EARTH

"Medicine Wheel" is a term that describes Native American stone circles used for prayer/ceremonial purposes. The stone circles of Europe can be understood to be the European version of a Medicine Wheel. Stone circles of Europe and Native American Medicine Wheels alike have been found to be aligned with solstices, equinoxes, cross quarter points (also called inter-cardinal), and certain stars or planets, showing that our ancient ancestors were in possession of Star Wisdom and a science of their own, and that they understood the relationship between Earth and Sky, inner and outer. If you are not comfortable with the term "Medicine Wheel" feel free to come up with another term of your own choosing.

Many years ago I had an interesting experience during a Full Moon ritual. We had just moved to a new home in the redwoods of Central California and were doing our first Full Moon ritual outdoors with some visiting Wiccan friends. As we proceeded with our ceremony I began to hear voices speaking, voices that became so loud that it was impossible for me to ignore them. I knew instantly it wasn't the neighbors. This was a different quality of sound than that which "carries" in the great outdoors.

Realizing this, I instinctively glanced over to where it was coming from, several yards away, further out in the yard and beneath some towering redwoods. There, with my inner vision, I saw some old people whom I knew to be Native American, standing and watching us, talking among themselves. As I gazed at them they became aware that I was taking notice of them. They began to talk to me, telling me they were the Grandmothers and Grandfathers of this area, telling me (with no small sense of impatience) how good it was that there were finally people here who were honoring the Old Ways and who could hear them when they spoke. They told me they had been waiting a long time for this to happen. With amazement, I communicated this to the friends who were present. The Grandfathers and Grandmothers then told me that we were to begin building and activating Medicine Wheels. "It is time," they said. I began asking questions—when, where, how. Their responses were "Start right now," and "Right here where we are standing!" and "Everywhere else you ever live." They told me it was important to do this because it was time to wake up the Earth.

This confused me, since I considered the Earth to already be awake. It was several years before I came to the realization that our "civilized" society, having forgotten how to be in relationship with Mother Earth, has forgotten also the art and science of creating and maintaining that relationship through the use of Sacred Sites and Stone Circles. Thus, the power flow cycle between ourselves and our Mother Planet has been seriously disrupted and must be properly reestablished. This power flow cycle feeds us, informs us, inspires us, and allows us to give back in kind to Earth. It keeps things balanced. Since it has been disrupted and we have forgotten how to be in this relationship, not only have we been "taking" from Earth largely without giving back, but we have simply forgotten how to allow Earth to communicate Herself to us, to inform us, to inspire us. Many power sites and stone circles thus have become dormant from lack of use. They are asleep. If we use them again, *and build new ones with the intention of relating to and communicating with our Mother Planet*, they will awaken. When they awaken they will "awaken us" (as Hunbatz Men, Mayan shaman and Daykeeper has told us), allowing the relationship to be reestablished, bringing back cellular memories (perhaps genetic "instincts") of how to be on and with the Earth.

The idea of creating new "sacred sites" is an important one (cautiously, though, as indicated in Chapter 2). This is not to dispute or ignore the power and value of places like Stonehenge, the Great Pyramid, or Chichen Itza. But the deeper lesson of my experience in the redwoods that Full Moon, was that it's not just about sacred sites and power spots. All of the Earth is sacred. Our assignment is to learn to be in touch with the sacred Earth in our very own locale.

RITUAL: BUILDING A MEDICINE WHEEL

This ritual is designed to address the issue of balance in a slightly different way than that illustrated just above. Rather than addressing our own inner Elements (which has been covered in preceding chapters) and their relationships to one another, it addresses the balance between our *Inner* Air, Fire, Water, and Earth and our *Outer* Elements—the Air, Fire, Water, and Earth of our Mother Earth. In performing this ritual, you will be addressing this relationship by means of a Stone Circle/Medicine Wheel.

You are going to build a Medicine Wheel/Stone Circle for the purposes of this ritual, so find a place outdoors that will be relatively undisturbed. If outside is not an option, indoors will do. Find a place inside, perhaps on your altar, where you can erect this Medicine Wheel of Earth and Self-Healing so that it will remain undisturbed indefinitely. Sometimes using very small stones and gluing them to a piece of cardboard is an option that can be used to create something permanent yet portable.

This Rite involves dance. Don't worry if you feel you are not a dancer. That's not the point. If you are physically handicapped, move as much of you as is possible to move, and create the dance with your intention and imagination.

Find five stones, designating one each for the Elements of Air, Fire, Water, and Earth, with the fifth stone for Spirit. In your chosen indoor or outdoor location, determine the position of the Four Directions. Create a Circle, with yourself, physically or imaginatively, in the center. This is your cosmos, your circle—and representative of the larger Cosmos and Circle of Life. You are the microcosm to the macrocosm of the Greater Circle of Life.

EAST

1. Sit in the center of your chosen Circle space. Breathe deeply for a few moments to settle in, and then do whatever you do to get yourself centered and grounded.

2. When you feel ready to begin, take up the stone for the East, walk over to the Eastern quarter of your Circle, and stand facing the East. Think for a while about the problems that Mother Earth's Air is having, such as pollution, holes in the ozone layer, and the resultant impact these things have on the rest of the beings of Earth. We all breathe the same Air, essentially. Allow your mind to rest on this for a few moments, long enough to "feel" the problems. Reflect for a bit about your Inner Air, your mental realm, and the problems you feel exist therein with regard to polluted versus clear thinking. Take another moment to feel how imbalance in your thinking impacts the rest of your life. This is a "sensing" process we are using here, rather than a strictly "thinking" one even though we are dealing with the Air/Mental Realm. Spend just a few moments on this. Don't be self-judgmental, just be aware of what needs healing and balancing within your mental realm. Reflect on how personal imbalances are related to collective imbalances, and how imbalanced Air/Mind in a group can collectively create an energy field where those imbalances physically manifest as an imbalanced world view or consciousness. Mass, or "herd" consciousness comes to mind as an example of such an imbalance.

3. Take a deep breath. Feel rising within you now a desire for these problems with the Inner and Outer Air to be healed, and feel your intention to bring this about. Let this desire and intention replace any sorrow/despair created within you by your previous imaging. Breathe out as you release all sorrow and despair. As you breathe in again, deeply, fill yourself with single-pointed intention to heal, so that you are breathing in this intention to heal and breathing out sorrow and despair. Do this until it feels complete, or until you decide it is as complete as it is going to be at this time.

4. Now envision representations of East, of the Element of Air. Picture the breezes blowing, causing the tree branches to sway and the leaves on the ground to swirl in little eddies. Picture the Sylphs dancing with the winds. Using the information about East and the Element of Air found in the preceding chapters, "see and feel" the Air Element in a clear and strong way.

5. Create a dance or song that is representative of the Element of Air, one that will align you with Air. It doesn't have to be a performance masterpiece; this is just something for yourself. Dance or sing facing East (continuing to hold the stone) with an awareness that you are contacting, invoking, and praying to the Element of Air. Dance or sing yourself into Air; become Air. And as you do so, become perfect, clean, free, pristine Air Element, the energetic template from which our physical, tangible Air springs into being.

6. Dance this now, dance Air; singing also if you desire, since movement and sound are both important factors with the Air Element. Let your dance take you all around the Circle, but especially from the East where you stand, into the Center of the Circle and back again. Weave, with the movement of your body, a connection between your Inner Air (represented by the Center of the Circle) and the Outer Air (represented by the East point of the Circle). As you are dancing Air, and weaving the Inner and Outer together, visualize

and send out strongly this sense of clean, pure Air, along with the prayer: "let the Airs be cleansed, be pure." Let your dance now become a fervent invocation of clean, pure Air—Inner and Outer. Let this feeling, and the exhilarating joyfulness of it, sweep through your body as you dance (and/or sing). Having allowed this surge of fervent, joyful invocation to fill you completely and even to excess, aim that part of it which overflows from you out into the world. Feel it surge forth from you, and picture again the clean, fresh Air. Picture it rushing forth from the place from which you have invoked it, and blowing through the places of Earth, sweeping away and transforming pollution, leaving only health, refreshment, and renewal in its wake.

7. When you feel complete with your dance, dance your way back to the Eastern portal. Lovingly, and with great strength of intention, place your stone upon the ground at the Place of the East. You have awakened and called forth the healing powers of the Air Element. Go back to the Center of the Circle and allow yourself to rest till you feel like moving on to the next part of the rite.

SOUTH

1. Take up the stone for the South and walk over to the Southern quarter of your Circle. Stand facing the South. Think for a while about the problems that Mother Earth's Fire is having (i.e., misuses of nuclear energy, species being rendered extinct, human tampering with Her creative power such as genetic manipulation), and the resultant impact these things have on the rest of the beings of Earth. Think about the fact that

Earth's soul and spirit have been so ignored and denied by "civilized" culture that, by extension, the souls and spirits of the beings in and on Her (and the spirit beings within her!) have also been feared, ignored, denied, or misinterpreted. Allow your mind to rest on these things for a few moments, long enough to "feel" the problems. Reflect for a moment about your Inner Fire, your Spiritual Self, and the problems you feel exist therein with regard to how you use or misuse your Inner Fires of passion, will, intention, creativity, and sexuality. Take another moment to feel how this imbalance impacts the rest of your life. Remember, this is a "sensing" process we are using, rather than a strictly "thinking" one.

2. Spend just a few moments on this. Once again, don't fall prey to harsh and useless self-judgment, just be aware of what it is within your spiritual, creative, passion-filled self that needs healing and balancing. Reflect on how personal imbalances (burning the candle at both ends, not tending your hearthfires physically, mentally, emotionally, or spiritually, misuse of sexual energy) are related to collective imbalances. See how imbalanced Fire/Spirit in a group can collectively create an energy field in which those imbalances become physically manifested as an imbalanced world (i.e., a society gone crazy with a need for eternal day and no night, with no respect for the creative power of sexuality or the sexual power of creativity).

3. Take a deep breath. Feel rising within you now a desire to heal these problems with the Inner and Outer Fire, and your intention to do so. Let this desire and intention replace any sorrow/despair created within you by

your previous imaging. Breathe deeply as you release all sorrow and despair, and fill yourself with passionate intention to heal.

4. Picture in your mind now the representations of South, of the Element of Fire. Picture the hearthfire burning comfortingly within your fireplace; feel the warmth and pleasure it provides. Envision the Hearth/Heartfires of the Earth glowing deep within Her in the form of Her molten, glowing, fiery core. Feel the warmth of the Sun, and see its brilliant light as it shines down upon you in midday strength. Imagine the stars at night, shining down upon you, and be aware not only that they are glowing balls of nuclear fusion , but that some Native Americans regarded them as the Campfires of the Ancestors, and thus, seeds of the future. Look again within the depths of your own hearthfire and see the Salamanders darting among the red-orange, glowing coals.

5. Create a dance or song that, for you, represents Fire, and that will align you with Fire. Dance or sing facing South (continuing to hold the stone) with an awareness that you are contacting, invoking, and praying to the Element of Fire. Dance or sing yourself into Fire: become Fire. As you do so, become perfect, clean, free, pristine Fire Element, the energetic template from which our physical, tangible Fire springs into being.

6. Dance this now, dance Fire; singing also if you like, knowing that movement is important with the Fire Element, just as it is with Air, though the movement can be of another type. Let your dance take you where it will, but especially from the South where you stand, into the Center of the Circle and back again, as you weave, with the movement of your body, a connection between your Inner Fire (represented by the Center of the Circle) and the Outer Fire (represented by the South point of the Circle). As you are dancing Fire, and weaving the Inner and Outer together, visualize and send out a strong sense of the purity of fire, along with the prayer: "Let the Fire be cleansed, be pure." Let your dance now become a fervent reconsecration of the blessed, purifying, transforming Fire, Inner and Outer. Let this feeling, the passionate joyfulness of it, sweep through your body as you dance (and/or sing). Having allowed this surge of fervent, joyful invocation/reconsecration to fill you completely and even to excess, aim that of it which overflows from you out into the world. Feel it surge forth from you, and picture again the pure, warming, transforming, blessing Fire. Picture it bursting forth from the place from which you have invoked it, and burning its way to each and every place where fire is misused on Earth or within us—purifying them, transforming them, blessing them, reconsecrating them to be in service to Life.

7. When you feel complete with your dance, dance your way back to the Southern portal. Lovingly, and with great strength of intention, place your stone upon the ground at the Place of the South. You have awakened and called forth the awesome creative and healing powers of the Fire Element. Go back to the Center of the Circle and allow yourself to rest till you feel like moving onto the next part of the rite.

WEST

1. Now take up the stone for the West and walk over to the Western quarter of your Circle. Stand facing the West. Think for a while about the problems that Mother Earth's Water is having (i.e., pollution from oil spills, toxic dumping, nuclear and other waste-filled barrels leaking) from being used, generally speaking, as a garbage dump. Think about the resultant impact these things have on the rest of the beings of Earth. Not just poor fish and dolphins; water flows and, like air, connects us all. Allow your mind to rest on this for just a moment, long enough to "feel" the problems. Reflect for a moment about your Inner Water, your emotional realm. How polluted are your Inner Waters? Do emotions stagnate inside of you, or do they flow through? Is stuck, non-flowing emotion usually allowed to build up to flood proportion within you? Floods can wreak havoc, and stagnation eventually creates toxicity. Are your Inner waters in danger of becoming toxic waste dumps similar to the way the Outer Waters have become? What kind of strange, mutated emotional creations will come to live in such polluted waters? And what about your physical "inner waters" in the form of your blood? Is your blood "toxic" from ill-nourishment in the form of chemically treated, unnatural foods? How can you be properly nourished, be it emotionally or physically, if the waters do not flow through correctly? If they are polluted or stagnant, and the channels that carry them are clogged with debris? Take another moment to feel how imbalance in your emotions impacts the rest of your life.

2. Spend a few moments on this, and as before, don't go into self-judgment. Just be aware of what within your emotional realm needs healing and balancing. Think about how emotions and thinking are tied together. Reflect on how personal imbalances are related to collective imbalances, and how imbalanced Water/Emotions in a group can contribute to a shared energy field where those imbalances can become physically manifested as an imbalanced world. Group hysteria comes to mind.

3. Take a deep breath. Feel rising within you now a desire to heal these problems with the Inner and Outer Water, and your intention to do so. Let this desire and intention replace any sorrow/despair created within you by your previous imaging. Breathe deeply as you release all sorrow and despair, and fill yourself with loving intention to heal.

4. Picture in your mind now the representations of West, of the Element of Water. Envision rain falling, cleansing, nourishing, and refreshing Earth's children. In your mind's eye, picture a river and follow its course as it flows to the sea. Picture the sea, with waves crashing onto the shore, and see the Undines dancing within the waves. Picture the Element and Direction as described in the previous chapters.

5. Create a dance or song that is representative of the Element of Water and that will align you with Water. Dance or sing facing West (continuing to hold the stone) with an awareness that you are contacting, invoking, and praying to the Element of Water. Dance or sing yourself into Water, become Water; and as you do so, become perfect,

clean, pure, precious, sparkling, pristine Water Element, the energetic template from which our physical, tangible Water springs into being.

6. Dance this now, dance Water. Sing also if you wish, a rhythmic chant of the sea, Primal Mother of Life, or a flowing, sinuous Riversong. Movement and sound are both appropriate. Let your dance take you all around the Circle, but especially from the West where you stand, into the Center of the Circle and back again. With your body's movement, weave a connection between your Inner Water (represented by the Center of the Circle) and the Outer Water (represented by the West point of the Circle). As you are dancing Water, and weaving the Inner and Outer together, visualize and put forth strongly the sense of clean, fresh, pure Water and the prayer "Let the Waters be cleansed, be pure." Let your dance now become a fervent invocation of clean, pure, nourishing Water, Inner and Outer. Let this feeling, and the flowing, crashing joyfulness of it, sweep through your body as you dance (and/or sing). Having allowed this surging wave of joyful invocation to fill you completely and to excess, aim that of it which overflows from you out into the world. Feel it rush forth from you, and picture again the crystalline clean, pure Water. Picture it rushing forth from the place from which you have invoked it, flowing through the Earth: cleansing, blessing, purifying, refreshing, nourishing as it goes, leaving only pristine cleanliness, health, and refreshment in its wake.

7. When you feel complete with your dance, dance your way back to the Western portal. Lovingly, and with great strength of inten-

tion, place your stone upon the ground at the Place of the West. You have awakened and called forth the cleansing and healing powers of the Water Element. Go back to the Center of the Circle and allow yourself to rest till you feel like moving on to the next part of the rite.

NORTH

1. Take up the stone for the North and walk over to the Northern quarter of your Circle. Think for a while about the problems that Mother Earth's soil and mineral kingdoms are having, such as pollution due to toxic chemicals used industrially and for farming, leakage from nuclear and other waste facilities, soil depletion and desertification due to tree removal and poor farming practices, greedy mining practices which remove large amounts of minerals, crystals, and other substances (especially uranium) that some Native peoples say are important to the correct balance of Earth's energy grid. Think about humanity's general lack of respect for "substance." Think about the resultant impact these things have on the rest of the beings of Earth. Allow your mind to rest on this for a few moments, long enough to "feel" the problems. Reflect for a moment about your Inner Earth—your physical body—and the problems you feel exist with regard to imbalances physically. Take another moment to feel how imbalance in your physical body such as ill health due to incorrect diet, toxicity of drug, alcohol, tobacco, or other substance abuse, and lack of exercise, impacts the rest of your life.

2. Spend a few moments reflecting on this, becoming aware of what it is within your physical realm that needs healing and balancing.

Realize here, that other factors also come into play with regard to physical ill health since the physical plane is the plane of manifestation for all the other planes of existence. Ill health can be a result of not only the above-mentioned causes, but also of karma from a previous life, genetic susceptibility, external factors such as epidemics and pollution, as well as imbalances within our mental, emotional, and spiritual selves. Reflect on how personal imbalances are related to collective imbalances, and how imbalanced Earth/Physical in a group collectively creates an energy field where those imbalances can become physically manifested as an imbalanced world. This is the most tangible of realms: Epidemics of contagious diseases come to mind.

3. Feel rising within you now a desire to heal these problems of the Inner and Outer Earth, and feel also your intention to do so. Let this desire and intention replace any sorrow/despair created within you by your previous imaging. Breathe deeply as you release all sorrow and despair, and fill yourself with determined intention to heal.

4. Picture in your mind now the representations of North, of the Element of Earth. Picture the mountains, the plains, the valleys. Picture the trees, the plants, the flowers, the animals. Imagine stones, crystals, bones. Envision the deep, dark, womblike caves, with stalactites and stalagmites growing from their rocky, crystal-studded walls and floors.

5. Create a dance or song for yourself that is representative of the Element of Earth, one that will align you with Earth. Dance or sing facing North (continuing to hold the stone) with an awareness that you are contacting, invoking, and praying to the Element of Earth. Dance or sing yourself into Earth—become Earth—and as you do so become perfect, clean, pristine Earth Element, the energetic template from which our physical, tangible Earth springs into being.

6. Dance and/or sing Earth now. Let your dance take you all around the Circle, but especially from the North where you stand, into the Center of the Circle and back again. With the movement of your body, weave a connection between your Inner Earth (represented by the Center of the Circle) and the Outer Earth (represented by the North point of the Circle). As you are dancing Earth, and weaving the Inner and Outer together, visualize and strongly send forth this sense of clean, unpolluted, pure Earth, along with the prayer: "Let the Earth be cleansed, be pure." Let your dance now become a fervent invocation of clean, pure Earth, Inner and Outer. Let this feeling, and the joyfulness of it, sweep through your body as you dance (and/or sing) this joyous reconsecration of the sacred pristine Earth. Having allowed this surge of fervent, joyful invocation to fill you completely and to excess, aim that part of it which overflows from you out into the world. Feel it move forth from you, and picture again the reconsecrated, unpolluted, clean, pristine Earth. Imagine the energy of this invocation/reconsecration pushing forth from the place from which you have invoked it, being born into the world and growing; sweeping away and transforming pollution, spreading itself regeneratively through all the places of Earth, and, like Brigit's mantle, covering the Earth with the fertile, healthy power of the Greening.

7. When you feel complete with your dance, dance your way back to the Northern portal. Lovingly, and with great strength of intention, place your stone upon the ground at the Place of the North. You have awakened and called forth the healing powers of the Earth Element. Go back to the Center of the Circle and allow yourself to rest till you feel like moving onto the next part of the rite.

CENTER

1. Stand now in the Center of your Circle. In every direction that you look, healing and transformation are taking place. Give thanks for the Powers and Beings of the Elements, and for the gift of Life. Close your eyes, and feel yourself rooting deeply into Mother Earth and simultaneously connecting into the Galactic center, "high" in the sky. Feel the energies of deep and high, Earth and Sky, run through your body, and know that you are a child of Earth and Sky, and serve as bridge between them. Feel the fire within you, in your "center" where the powers of Earth and Sky meet, burning brightly. Place the remaining stone in the Center of your Circle, with an awareness of yourself as the Balance Point/Center of the Circle, your conscious choices making a difference in both the Inner World and the Outer World.

2. When you feel complete, give thanks again, and declare your rite ended.

3. Perform this rite again as you feel it to be necessary.

You have created a sacred space, a Medicine Wheel/Stone Circle that now may be used for further ritual, healing, and prayer. When you are feeling upset or imbalanced within, go to your Medicine Wheel to rebalance and heal yourself, invoking whichever Element you feel is necessary to put you back into balance again. When you do this, imagine yourself to be in the center of your Medicine Wheel circle, facing the direction of your "excess" element. Reach your hands out and take up the "excess," turn to the opposite side and offer it as a gift to the opposite direction. Then simply stand quietly, breathing deeply and slowly, feeling your energies shift until you feel more balanced. Reach your hands out in the direction of your "deficient" element, to receive what is offered to you. If nothing is offered to you from a particular direction, be aware that your situation is more complex than you perceive, and simply request, and be open to receive, the healing/balancing that you need.

SOME FINAL WORDS

Many of us living in this modern era feel lost. We may have good, fulfilling jobs, nice homes, lots of electronic gadgets to play with, the latest movies for our VCRs, enough money to buy books like this. Yet there is an emptiness inside that we are finding hard to fill. We read book after book, take class after class, have relationship after relationship—trying to fill this emptiness. But it is an emptiness of spirit, and cannot be filled by reading a book, taking a class, or having a relationship. These things may produce a temporary cessation of the symptoms; they may stimulate us mentally, physically, or emotionally. They may even point us in a direction that is good for us to take. But often we mistake the map for the destination itself.

The state of the world—the environment, the homeless, our children—troubles us. We see the same maladies almost everywhere we look. If Spirit is all around, if it does indeed permeate all, why is it then that so many of us experience such emptiness of Spirit? The reason is that we have largely lost touch with our ways of connecting into and feeling the presence of Spirit (as well as "spirits"). Spirit didn't go anywhere, we did. We turned our attention elsewhere, and forgot how to turn back. Sometimes this losing touch of the ways of connecting with Spirit is the result of what shamanic practitioners refer to as "soul loss" or "soul fragmentation." As our lives unfold, emotional trauma sometimes causes parts of our soul to fragment and depart, somewhat like a scared child who runs and hides. Without these missing fragments we are not whole; we do not possess and cannot utilize all our ability to fully connect into, feel the presence of, and participate in the spiritual dimension of our existence. And if we cannot be present with and participate in the spiritual dimension of our existence, participation in our physical existence becomes flat, one dimensional, and meaningless.

Can we even see the connection here between the fragmentation happening within ourselves and that of our Mother Planet? Forests cut down, species extinct, air and water polluted, holes in the ozone layer—can we *feel* this connection between ourselves and our precious planet?

We've lost touch with the Spirit within ourselves and our world. We've lost touch with the Spirits of our ancestors, who once held the wisdom of our tribes and could be called upon for guidance and help. We've lost touch with our Spirit allies and helpers, those beings who subtly assist us from the other realms. We've lost touch with the spirits of the land, the plants, the animals, the Sun, the Moon, and the Stars.

Our materialistic culture and science has taught that none of these exist: there is no Spirit within, the Moon is a dead rock, and the Sun is just a glowing ball of gases. If we just quantify, count, and observe behavior, we will then know the essence of the thing. Even our moods and behavior patterns have quantifiable, genetic basis, they tell us. So we define ourselves by our quantifiable characteristics, behaviors, and even our possessions—and are under the mistaken impression that we know ourselves well. We remember the things that occur in our lives and mistakenly think that we are only the sum of our memories. Yet all the while the emptiness, and the longing to fill it, remains.

We take a walk in the forest, and are filled with peace. We come back refreshed, renewed, and inspired. The beauty of the setting has refreshed our weary souls, the hues of nature have nourished us. Without realizing it, we have connected with the presence of both Spirit and spirits. This very natural occurrence, in a very natural setting, has made all the difference in the world. It happens to most of us so rarely, and when it does we seldom understand quite what it really was that just happened to us. Yet it is our natural inheritance! We are *part* of nature, *meant* to be in contact with, and interacting with, the rest of our natural family. When we are connected in this way, we do not feel alone because we are not alone: We are surrounded by thousands of plants, animals, Devas, Nature Spirits, Elemental spirits, and Faeries—our relatives!

Like Dorothy, who though surrounded by the distracting splendors of the Emerald City desired only to go home, we also must decide to go home. I'm not suggesting we all try to move into the wilderness; only that we work at reestablishing our relationship with our home planet and our many relatives, including our invisible relatives such as Devas, Nature Spirits, and Faeries. In this book I have offered my humble suggestions toward reestablishing awareness of and conscious contact with the Elemental Realms as a way towards reintegrating ourselves into the natural flow of life. There are other ways to approach this "refocusing" we need to do; anything that works for you is the right way to do it.

Things are such in the world today that we can no longer afford the illusion of separation from the rest of nature. We can no longer deny we are part of the web of existence, or that what happens on our part of the web affects other parts of the web. And we have to *live* this, not just mentally subscribe to it as an appealing idea. When we do, our world opens up and out to us in a profound way. No longer do we feel empty; rather, we quite tangibly *feel* ourselves permeated with Spirit. No longer do we feel alone; rather, we now can feel our interconnectedness with every other life form. We fill with joy and gratitude for the love and support that constantly surrounds and upholds us.

Separation or Connection? Which are we going to choose?

APPENDICES

Great Beings
of the Directions

The following are some of the names/designations of the Four Great Beings of the Directions, drawn from a small sampling of other spiritual traditions. In general, these Beings were seen to be the four pillars of heaven, holding up the four corners of the sky, or else they were seen to be the "Keepers" of the four pillars or gateways of the heavens.

JUDEO-CHRISTIAN:

East/Air: Raphael
South/Fire: Michael
West/Water: Gabriel
North/Earth: Uriel

These are the four, great archangels of Judeo-Christian tradition and medieval/Renaissance magical tradition.

NORSE:

North—Northri
East—Ostri
South—Suthri
West—Vestri

These are the Four Dwarves who hold up the dome of the sky, one at each of the four cardinal directions. Their names are those of the direction itself: Northri (or Nordri, meaning "away, below"), Sudri (meaning "the brilliant"), Ostri (or Austri, meaning "glowing, bright, burning"), and Vestri (referring to "evening, night").

ICELANDIC:

Northeast—dragon
South—rock giant brandishing an iron staff
West—huge bird
Southeast—powerful bull

CHINESE:

Green Dragon of the *East*
Red Bird of the *South*
White Tiger of the *West*
Black Tortoise (or Dark Warrior) of the *North*

These are traceable back at least as far as the Han Dynasty of 206 BC–220 AD, but are probably older. These are the Four Cosmic Animals of the Chinese Tradition, associated with four zones along the celestial equator, and were equated with the four seasons. (Krupp, *Echoes of the Ancient Skies,* page 112)

EGYPTIAN:

East—Duametef, Fire God
West—Qebehsenuf, Air God
South—Imset, Water God
North—Hapi, Earth God

CHEROKEE:

East—the Red Man (of the Sun Land), first created and most important, he signified the Sun
South—the White man, man of purity and peace
West—the Black Man (of the Darkening Land) who was named "fearless"

North—the Blue Man (of the Frigid Land)

These beings were seen as agents of the Supreme Beings and mediators between them and creation. Each of them were given power over the world.

Some Cherokee lore mentions Beings called the *Adawees*. They are said to be Wise Protectors, Guardians of the Directions, and Gateways of Consciousness.

SKIDI PAWNEE:

East—the Yellow Star (Capella)
North—the White Star (Sirius)
West—the Big Black Meteoric Star (Vega)
South—the Red Star (Antares)

These stars were considered by the Skidi Pawnee of Nebraska's great plains to be the pillars of heaven: the four stars whose hands supported the sky while their feet were firmly planted on the ground. The Skidi seemingly placed greater value on the intercardinal directions of Northwest, Southwest, Northeast, Southeast, than on the cardinal directions of ESWN. The above stars marked these intercardinal directions, but served the function of "Guardians of the Directions." Each of the eight directions had a particular tree, animal, season, time of life, phenomenon of weather, and color associated with them, in addition to the associated star.

MAYAN:

East—the Kan Bacab; associated with the color yellow
South—the Ek Bacab; associated with the color black
West—the Chac Bacab; associated with the color red
North—the Zac Bacab; associated with the color white

These are the Bacabs, the four huge Iguanas or Bees said to hold up the sky.

This next one does not really qualify as being descriptive of, or as *naming* the Four Great Beings of the Directions, but does deal with the Four Directions, their respective "tools," and the Four Elements.

CELTIC:

The Four Cities spoken of by writer Fiona Macleod are:
Gorias in the *East*
Finias in the *South*
Murias in the *West*
Falias in the *North*

The Tuatha De Danaan were said to have come from these cities, or "convocations," bringing with them the Sword of Nuada from Gorias; the Spear of Lugh from Finias; the Cauldron of the Dagda from Murias; and the Stone of Destiny from Falias. The four tools link their respective cities to the Four Elements.

Meditations
and Rituals

JOURNEY TO THE GUARDIANS OF THE ELEMENTS

For this journey build an altar dedicated to the Element whose Guardian you wish to contact. See the relevant chapter for information on building the altar. If you are not able to physically build the altar, then build it in your imagination and feel yourself to be surrounded by representations of that particular element. Spend some time reviewing the Elemental Meditation included in the appropriate chapter, till you are quite familiar with the terrain, setting, and feeling, and can call them up at will. When you have done this, you are ready to begin the journey.

Begin by following the usual pre-journey suggestions of relaxation, deep breathing, etc. Then visualize yourself traveling into the Elemental realm and being surrounded by the manifestations of the Element as portrayed in the Elemental meditations in Chapters 2–5 (in this journey, you do not have to follow exactly the steps given in the Elemental meditation journey unless you want to; the important thing is to be able to place yourself, with the use of your inner senses, within the Elemental Realm as clearly as possible). When you feel that you are clearly and definitely present within this Elemental Realm, respectfully request that you be granted an audience with the Guardian Spirit of this Element, and be ready to meet with this Great Being however it may appear to you. Listen carefully to what you are told, ask questions if you think it appropriate, and don't forget to express your thanks for the opportunity to speak with this Being and enter its realms. When you are finished, turn back and return the way you came, allowing enough time to thoroughly return to present time and place.

Basic Circle Casting

This requires a tiny taper candle, a Center candle, two larger taper candles, and one candle for each of the Four Directions (tapers or votives). Begin with a few moments of silence and slow, calm, deep breathing. When you are ready to begin, bring your attention to the Center point of the Circle. Use a match to light the Center Candle and say:

By the power of the Ancient Providence,
which was forever and is forever;
which is all knowing, wise, loving, and becoming;
which is male and female, God and Goddess,
Do I light this candle, Symbol of the All
encompassing, Ever-Becoming Presence.

From this Center candle, light the tiny taper candle. Now rest your attention on the two taper candles, and lighting them with the tiny taper candle, say:

From the One comes the Two,
I give greetings and honor
To the Goddess and the God,
Our Mother and our Father.

Again, using the tiny taper, light the candles of the Four Directions, saying:

From the Two come the Many.
I give greetings and honor to the Old Ones,
The Powers of Air, Fire, Water and Earth.

As you say the words Air, Fire, Water, and Earth, bring your awareness strongly to these powers, and to their respective places of East, South, West, and North. As you do this, imagine energy flowing out of the Center and toward the East, then toward the South, then West, then North, and around to the East again. If you wish, you may visualize this energy as ribbons of glowing golden or blue-white light.

If you plan to use the physical elements in your ceremony, you must now bless them. So lifting up the bowl of incense, say:

Creature of Air, be blessed and pure; Purify my Sacred Circle with your pleasing perfume, and carry my prayers to the Great Ones.

Placing your hands on either side of the flame of either the Center Candle or of the God and Goddess candles, say:

Spark of Fire, spark of life; bless me with your power; I bless you with my love.

Lift up the cup of water and say:

Child of Sea, of River, of Stream, be clean, be pure, be blessed. Cleanse and bless me, refresh and make me new again.

Lifting up the bowl of salt (cornmeal or earth), say:

Substance of Earth, let all that is not clean be cleansed, all that is not pure be purified, all that no longer serves, be transmuted. Bless me with your power of transmutation.

You may want to sprinkle yourself with a few drops of water, a few grains of the salt, waft yourself with the incense, and allow yourself to feel the heat of the candle flame, as part of this process. Then proceed on to the rest of your working.

CIRCLE OF PROTECTION

When making the inner journeys suggested in this book, if you do not wish to work within a formal magical Circle, the following simple Circle may be used instead.

You are the Center of your own Circle, so begin by determining where each Direction is in your chosen locale. Note these for yourself, even so simply as to note that "East is over there by the doorway," or window or wherever. Sit comfortably in your chosen place, the center of your own simple Circle, eyes closed, and allow yourself to breathe slowly and deeply for a few moments till you feel relaxed and at ease.

As you continue to breathe slowly and deeply, feel yourself filling with the glowing light of Spirit. Breathe it into yourself. Arise now, and walk in a circle around your chair or seat, creating a protective boundary for yourself, saying (and see this with your inner vision as you say it) as you do so:

"I weave into being around myself, a Circle of Radiant Light; guarding me, protecting me; keeping out all harm, allowing in only that which is true and is of service. In the many names of the Lady and the Lord do I create this Circle."

When you have finished this return to your seat.

Turn your attention now to the East, or if you prefer, stand and face each direction as you do this, and call upon the Great Being of the East (by whatever name you choose to use, or simply as "Guardian of the Air Realms"). Ask this Being to be here with you, to guard your Circle, to lend aid to what you are about to do. Make this request simply and graciously, and in your own words. Do not command this Being's presence. End by thanking this Being for his/her presence and assistance. Repeat this at each of the other Directions (in clockwise order): South, West, North.

You have now created your sacred space, and may do your meditations/inner journeys within it. When you are finished, turn your attention once again to the Great Beings who have been with you, guarding and protecting your Circle. Thank them again for their presence and assistance and bid them farewell. Now arise from your seat and "unwind" your Circle, this time moving in a counterclockwise direction (East, North, West, South, and back to the East), saying:

"By the power of the Lady and the Lord do I unwind this Circle and return its elements to their places of origin."

Visualize yourself drawing this energy back into you. Visualize it flowing through you, then spiraling out of you again, back to its cosmic source.

Recipes

Earth Element

Dragon Bone Biscuits

3 to 4 tablespoons cold water

1/4 teaspoon salt

1/2 teaspoon baking soda

1 1/2 cups flour

1/2 cup Dragon Bone powder

1/2 cup butter, softened

Mix together all the dry ingredients, then mix in the softened butter. Add as much water as necessary to make a biscuit-consistency dough. Roll out into finger shapes about 2 inches long, and work with the ends a bit till they resemble bones. Bake at 350° F for about 10 minutes. Makes approximately 12 biscuits.

Earth and Air Elements

Strong Bone Tea

Nettles

Oatstraw

Place a good-sized handful of each of these herbs in a quart jar and cover with boiling water. Allow to steep for 10 minutes or so to make a tea, or 4 hours to make an infusion (longer steeping enhances medicinal qualities). Strain and serve.

This tea strengthens the bones and calms the nerves.

Earth and Water Elements

This soup recipe is one of those that defies exact quantities. Here's a recipe for a fairly large amount.

Sea Soup

seaweeds (kelp, wakame, sea lettuce, dulse, nori)

tamari soy sauce

daikon (white radish)

shiitake mushrooms

clams, shrimp, scallops, and other seafood

garlic

green onion

salt

Fill a pot with about 3 to 4 quarts of water and heat. Add 3 or 4 strips of kelp (about 4 inches in length). Some stores sell kelp under its Japanese name of kombu. Let this boil for a few minutes. Add about 1/4 cup of tamari soy sauce. Then chop up the daikon (fairly thin) and shiitake mushrooms and throw them into the pot. Allow this to cook till the daikon is soft (about 5 to 10 minutes), then add 2 pieces of wakame, approximately 3 inches square. Add whatever seafood you wish (I use shrimp, clams, and scallops), along with 2 to 3 cloves of garlic and 1/2 bunch chopped green onions. Turn down the heat to a simmer. Cook for another 5 to 10 minutes. Try not to overcook the seafood. Add salt or more tamari to taste, and serve.

Sea vegetables, which possess astonishing quantities of minerals, make this soup quite mineral rich and nourishing to blood and bones. Shiitake mushrooms are known to have properties that inhibit tumor formation, daikon is said to help disperse congestion, and garlic is a natural antibiotic/antiseptic.

FIRE ELEMENT

"Kill the Chill" Soup

1 cup black beans
6 cups water
2 carrots, chopped
2 stalks celery, chopped
1/2 cabbage or kale, chopped
2 to 3 cloves of garlic, chopped coarsely
2 medium onions, chopped
3 to 4 thin slices of fresh ginger
salt, tamari, pepper to taste

Cook the black beans in the water (you may need more water if you use a pressure cooker). Or you can use canned black beans and an appropriate amount of water to make your soup broth. Chop the carrots, celery, and cabbage and toss them into the pot with the cooked beans. Add water if necessary. Sauté the garlic, onions, and ginger and add them to the soup pot. Let all this simmer till the veggies are well cooked and the tastes have blended. Season to taste.

This soup is mineral rich and very warming. It nourishes the inner fires in many ways.

Winter Morning Breakfast Porridge

2 cups water
1 cup cornmeal
1 cup milk (dairy, soy, or coconut milk)
1/2 teaspoon salt
1/4 teaspoon ground cinnamon
1/4 teaspoon cardamom
1/8 teaspoon ginger
sprinkle of powdered cloves, if desired

Mix 1 cup of water with the cornmeal and stir to dissolve lumps. Place the milk and remaining water in a saucepan along with the salt, and allow to heat gently. When it gets very warm, stir in the cornmeal/water and stir well. Keep stirring until it thickens. When this happens, cover quickly and turn the heat to a very low simmer. Allow the porridge to simmer for 5 to 10 minutes, stirring occasionally. Be aware that this mixture has a tendency to spatter upwards at you when you lift the cover, so be careful. About half way through the cooking time, stir in the spices. Raisins or other dried fruit can be added to this if desired, either while cooking or after. This porridge may be served as is, or with milk, or butter and maple syrup. Lightly toasted, chopped walnuts, pecans, or almonds may be added as a nice topping.

This porridge is delicious, warming, and has a fair amount of protein: a good way to start a winter day.

Bibliography

Agrippa, Henry Cornelius. *Three Books of Occult Philosophy or Magic.* Willis Whitehead, ed. Chicago, IL: Hahn & Whitehead, 1898.

Apuleus. *The Golden Ass,* trans. by Robert Graves. NY: Farrar, Straus and Giroux, 1951.

Ashe, Geoffrey. *Dawn Behind the Dawn.* NY: Henry Holt & Co, 1992.

Bord, Janet and Colin. *The Secret Country.* London, England: Paladin Books, Granada Publ. Ltd., 1978.

Bruyere, Rosalyn L. *Wheels of Light.* Sierra Madre, CA: Bon Productions, 1989.

Crowther, Patricia. *Lid Off the Cauldron.* York Beach, ME: Samuel Weiser Inc., 1981.

Dames, Michael. *Mythic Ireland.* London, England: Thames and Hudson, Ltd., 1992.

Farrar, Stewart. *What Witches Do.* Custer, WA: Phoenix Publishing, 1991.

Frawley, David, O.M.D. *Ayurvedic Healing, a Comprehensive Guide.* Salt Lake City, UT: Passage Press, 1989.

Graves, Tom. *Needles of Stone Revisited.* Glastonbury, Somerset, England: Gothic Image Publications, 1978 and 1986.

Gray, William. *Magical Ritual Methods.* London, England: Helios Books, 1971.

Gray, William. *Inner Traditions of Magic.* London, England: Aquarian Press, 1971.

Griggs, Barbara. *Green Pharmacy.* Rochester, VT: Healing Arts Press, 1981.

Grimm, Jacob. *Teutonic Mythology* (in four volumes). NY: Dover Publications, Inc., 1966, republication from work published by George Bell and Sons, 1883.

Gurudas, *Gem Elixirs and Vibrational Healing, Vol. I,* Boulder, CO: Cassandra Press, 1985.

Huson, Paul. *Mastering Herbalism.* NY: A Scarborough Book, Stein & Day Publishers, 1975.

Judith, Anodea. *Wheels of Light: A User's Guide to the Chakra System.* St. Paul, MN: Llewellyn Publications, 1987.

Krupp, Dr. E.C. *Echoes of the Ancient Skies: The Astronomy of Lost Civilizations.* NY: Harper & Row Publishers, 1983.

Lad, Vasant. *Ayurveda, the Science of Self-Healing.* Santa Fe, NM: Lotus Press, 1984.

MacDonald, Lorraine. "A'Gaot: The Wind and The Airts in Gaelic Folklore," *Dalriada Magazine,* (Feb. 1996)

Maciocia, Giovanni. *Foundations of Chinese Medicine.* NY: Churchill Livingstone, 1989.

Matthews, Caitlin. *Elements of the Celtic Tradition.* Longmead, Shaftesbury, Dorset, England: Element Books, Ltd., 1989.

Matthews, Caitlin. *Singing the Soul Back Home.* Longmead, Shaftesbury, Dorset, England: Element Books, Ltd., 1995.

Matthews, John. *The Celtic Shaman: A Handbook.* Longmead, Shaftesbury, Dorset, England: Element Books, Ltd., 1991.

Purce, Jill. *The Mystic Spiral: Journey of the Soul.* NY: Thames and Hudson, 1974.

Rockwell, David. *Giving Voice to Bear.* West Cork, Ireland: Roberts Rinehart Publishers, 1991.

Starck, Marcia. *Earth Mother Astrology.* St. Paul, MN: Llewellyn Publications, 1989.

Stewart, R.J. *Music and the Elemental Psyche.* Rochester, VT: Destiny Books, a division of Inner Traditions, International, 1987.

Stewart, R.J. *Music, Power, Harmony.* London, England: Blandford, an imprint of Cassel, 1990.

Stewart, R.J. *The Prophetic Vision of Merlin.* London, England: Arkana, an imprint of Routledge and Kegan Paul, 1986 .

Sun Bear & Wabun. *The Medicine Wheel: Earth Astrology.* Englewood Cliffs, NJ: Prentice-Hall, Inc., 1980.

Sun Bear, Wabun Wind, and Chrysalis Mulligan. *Dancing with the Wheel.* NY: a Fireside Book, Simon & Schuster, 1991.

Teeguarden, Iona Marsaa. *Acupressure Way of Health: Jin Shin Do.* Tokyo & NY: Japan Publications, Inc., 1978.

Tindall, Gillian. *A Handbook on Witches.* London, England: Arthur Barker Ltd., 1965.

Valiente, Doreen. *An ABC of Witchcraft Past and Present.* NY: St. Martin's Press, 1973.

Weed, Susun. *Menopausal Years: The Wisewoman Way.* Woodstock, NY: Ashtree Publishing, 1992.

Zimmerman, J.E. *Dictionary of Classical Mythology.* NY: Bantam Books, 1964.

SUGGESTED READINGS

Beyerl, Paul. *Master Book of Herbalism.* Custer, WA: Phoenix Publishing, Inc., 1984.

Bruyere, Rosalyn L. *Wheels of Light.* Sierra Madre, CA: Bon Productions, 1989.

Cowan, Elliot. *Plant Spirit Medicine.* Newburg, OR: Swan-Raven & Co., 1995.

Cunningham, Scott. *Cunningham's Encyclopedia of Magical Herbs.* St. Paul, MN: Llewellyn Publications, 1985.

Cunningham, Scott. *Magical Herbalism.* St. Paul, MN: Llewellyn Publications, 1982.

Gray, William. *Magical Ritual Methods.* London, England: Helios Books, 1971.

Gray, William. *Inner Traditions of Magic.* London, England: Aquarian Press, 1970.

Meadows, Kenneth. *Where Eagles Fly.* Shaftsbury, Dorset, England: Element Books, 1995.

O'Cathain, Seamas. *The Festival of Brigit.* Blackrock, Co. Dublin, Ireland: DBA Publications, Ltd., 1995.

Rockwell, David. *Giving Voice to Bear.* West Cork, Ireland: Roberts Rinehart Publishers, 1991.

Starck, Marcia. *Healing with Astrology.* Freedom, CA: The Crossing Press, 1997.

Sun Bear & Wabun. *The Medicine Wheel: Earth Astrology.* Englewood Cliffs, NJ: Prentice-Hall, Inc., 1980.

Sun Bear, Wabun Wind, and Chrysalis Mulligan. *Dancing with the Wheel.* NY: a Fireside Book, Simon & Schuster, 1991.

Storm, Hyemeyohsts. *Lightningbolt.* NY: A One World Book, Ballantine Books, 1994.

Tierra, Michael. *Planetary Herbology.* Santa Fe, NM: Lotus Press, 1988.

Index

RELATED BOOKS FROM THE CROSSING PRESS

An Astrological Herbal for Women

By Elisabeth Brooke

An extensive guide to the use of herbs in healing the mind, body and spirit, organized by planetary influence. Includes the astrological significance of 38 common herbs, as well as their physical, emotional, and ritual uses.

$12.95 • Paper • ISBN 0-89594-740-41

Casting the Circle: A Women's Book of Ritual

By Diane Stein

A comprehensice guide including 23 full rituals for waxing, full, and waning moons, the eight Sabats, and rites of passage.

$14.95 • Paper • ISBN 0-89594-411-1

The Goddess Celebrates: An Anthology of Women's Rituals

Contributors include Z. Budapest, Starhawk, and others.

"...this collection will stimulate discussion among readers interested in women's spirituality."
—*Booklist*

$14.95 • Paper • ISBN 0-89594-460-X

Pocket Guide to Celtic Spirituality

By Sirona Knight

The Earth-centered philosophy and rituals of ancient Celtic spirituality have special relevance today as we strive to balance our relationship with the planet. This guide offers a comprehensive introduction to the rich religious tradition of the Celts.

$6.95 • Paper • ISBN 0-89594-907-5

Pocket Guide to Shamanism

By Tom Cowan

Are you intrigued by the mysteries of nature and the realm of the spirit? Have you experienced a magical or mystical occurrence? Perhaps shamanism is calling you. Bringing shamanism into your life can allow you to restore sacred ritual, gain insight, and live with sensitivity and respect for the planet.

$6.95 • Paper • ISBN 0-89594-845-1

Pocket Guide to Wicca

By Paul Tuitean & Estelle Daniels

Wicca is a modern version of an ancient pagan sacred tradition that predated Christianity. It is Earth-, Nature-, and Fertility-oriented. This guide provides a comprehensive introduction to anyone interested in "the Craft".

$6.95 • Paper • ISBN 0-89594-904-0

Shamanism as a Spiritual Practice for Daily Life

By Tom Cowan

This inspirational book blends elements of shamanism with inherited traditions and contemporary religious commitments. "An inspiring spiritual call."   —*Booklist*

$16.95 • Paper • ISBN 0-89594-838-9

The Wiccan Path: A Guide for the Solitary Practitioner

By Rae Beth

This is a guide to the ancient path of the village wisewoman. Writing in the form of letters to two apprentices, Rae Beth provides rituals for the key festivals of the wiccan calendar. She also describes the therapeutic powers of trancework and herbalism, and outlines the Pagan approach to finding a partner.

$12.95 • Paper • ISBN 0-89594-744-7

A Wisewoman's Guide to Spells, Rituals, and Goddess Lore

By Elisabeth Brooke

Gathering together for the very first time all the disciplines of European witchcraft and giving rituals and spells for us to use, this is a remarkable compendium of magical lore, psychic skills and women's mysteries.

$12.95 • Paper • 0-89594-779-X

A Woman's I Ching

By Diane Stein

Finally, a feminist interpretation of the popular ancient text for divining the character of events. Stein's version reclaims the feminine, or yin, content of the ancient work and removes all oppressive language and imagery. Her interpretation envisions a healing world in which women can explore different roles free from the shadow of patriarchy.

$16.95 • Paper • ISBN 0-89594-857-5

To receive a current catalog from The Crossing Press,
please call toll-free, 800-777-1048.
Visit our Website on the Internet at: www.crossingpress.com